Portland Commur

VIRUS

THE CO-DISCOVERER
OF HIV TRACKS ITS
RAMPAGE AND CHARTS
THE FUTURE

Luc Montagnier

translated from the French

by Stephen Sartarelli

W · W · Norton & Company

New York   London

For information about permission to reproduce selections from this book, write to
Permissions, W. W. Norton & Company, Inc., 500 Fifth Avenue, New York, NY 10110

The text of this book is composed in 12.5/14 Perpetua
with the display set in Felix Titling MT and Perpetua
Composition and manufacturing by The Haddon Craftsmen, Inc.
Book design by Margaret M. Wagner

Library of Congress Cataloging-in-Publication Data
Montagnier, Luc.
[Virus et des hommes. English]
Virus : the co-discoverer of HIV tracks its rampage and charts the future / by Luc
Montagnier; translated from French by Stephen Sartarelli.
p.   cm.
Translation of: Des virus et des hommes.
Includes bibliographical references and index.
ISBN 0-393-03923-4
1. HIV infections—Etiology—Research—History. 2. HIV (Viruses)—Research—
History. I. Title.
QR201.A37M66 1999
616.97'92—dc21   99-19650
                                                            CIP

W. W. Norton & Company, Inc.
500 Fifth Avenue, New York, N.Y. 10110
www.wwnorton.com

W. W. Norton & Company Ltd.
10 Coptic Street, London WC1A 1PU

1 2 3 4 5 6 7 8 9 0

VIRUS

Contents

5

6   Contents

Acknowledgments

❧ SCIENTIFIC discoveries are often a matter of circumstance and chance. This was true in Pasteur's time, and is equally so in ours, as we have seen with the discovery of the AIDS virus.

I would like here to thank all those colleagues who accompanied me on this adventure, in difficult moments as in times of hope. Without them, none of this work could have been achieved.

A special thought goes out for Jacqueline Gruest, who passed away before her time.

I also cannot forget BRU, LAI, LOI, and all the others, all those patients whose initials have become familiar to us. Their trust in us was firm from the very beginning. There are others, too, who prefer to remain anonymous. They have always been present in my thoughts; my heartfelt gratitude and compassion goes out to them.

I would like to thank Caroline Chaine, whose assistance and perseverance have made the realization of the present book possible; Sophie Chamaret, who was kind enough to lend a critical reading to this story, in which she herself played an active part; Marie-Lise Gougeon, Gustavo Gonzalez, and Marc Girard, who agreed to reread certain chapters of this book; and

Jean-Luc Fidel of Editions Odile Jacob, who was lavish in his advice and assistance.

I would also like to thank Marie-Noëlle Dehoux and Edith Martin, who saw to the typewriting of this text; Stephen Sartarelli for providing the English version of the book; and Dr. Emily Carrow for her invaluable help in the preparation of the English language edition.

Introduction

If human civilization lasts, if it continues to spread, infectious diseases will increase in number in every region of the globe. Exchanges and migrations will bring the human and animal diseases of all regions to every country. The work is already well advanced; its future is assured.

—CHARLES NICOLLE, The Destiny of Infectious Diseases, 1932

⟡ THIS prediction by Charles Nicolle, director of the Pasteur Institute of Tunis and discoverer of the vector of typhus, has unfortunately come true. AIDS has invaded our society, shaken our prejudices and beliefs, and raised the question of world solidarity. In 1998 alone there were 5.8 million people newly infected with HIV; there are now 34 million people living with HIV/AIDS.[1]

The epidemic is still spreading fast in many countries of all continents, sometimes taking an explosive mode, such as in South Africa, Zimbabwe, Zambia, India, Cambodia, and southern China. Every day, 6,000 children become infected.

The best defense against this new scourge is prevention and research.

Researchers have from the beginning been at the forefront of the battle against AIDS, and very quickly gained important successes. The disease was identified in 1981, and two years later the causal agent was isolated for the first time. Blood tests were available by 1985, which almost entirely eliminated the transmission of HIV by blood and blood products. In 1987, the first viral inhibitor, AZT, was shown to have short-term efficacy on disease progression. In 1994, it proved to reduce considerably the transmission of HIV from mother to child. In 1996, for the first time, a combination of three viral inhibitors, including a protease inhibitor, was shown to reduce viral multiplication by 1,000 times while dramatically improving the patient's condition.

However much remains to be done. Triple-drug therapy does not cure the patient of infection. The virus still persists in the body. Toxic effects are frequent, as are mutant viral strains resistant to treatment. And ninety percent of HIV-infected patients, mostly from poor countries, do not have access to the benefits of antiviral drugs, due to inadequate health-care programs compounded by the expense of effective treatments.

Therefore, more than ever, a worldwide effort is necessary for controlling the epidemic. This book has the ambition of contributing to this effort by informing the reader of the complex situation in nontechnical language. Part I gives a vivid history of the virus's discovery, as it was lived by the author. It is a personal vision, yet with the intent of giving an objective rendering of the events and the people who shaped them in this pioneering period of medical history. Parts II and III give an overview of our current knowledge (as of 1998) of the virus and the disease. More technical aspects appear as notes at the end of the book. Finally, Part IV addresses the new frontiers of research and the prospects for better treatments, especially vaccines.

Vaccine, a magic word, is still a dream for AIDS researchers. Only with the continued dedication and creativity of the research community, combined with an extraordinary commitment from government and private citizens, will that dream become a reality.

A global problem must receive a global solution!

I

DISCOVERY

1

The Accidents of Research

CHILDHOOD ACCIDENT

~&~ NORTH of Poitiers, France, National Highway 10 emerges from the sharp bluffs of the Clain Valley on its way toward a plateau bordered by small hills. This is the ancient boundary between northern and southern France, not far from the point at which the advancing Saracen invaders were stopped, at the gateway to Queen Eleanor's beloved Aquitaine. A bit farther on, before Châtellerault, the red Roman roof tiles give way to Angevin slate, and the singsong accent of the Poitou region is eclipsed by the purity of Touraine speech. Once past these hills, the highway doglegs down into the valley of what is no longer but a feeble stream, the Auxance. There, well tucked away, lies the village of Grand-Pont.

The front-wheel-drive vehicle is rolling along at a high speed, the driver feeling almost surprised at the ease with which the car hugs the road, handling the sharpest curves with no difficulty at all. It is a clear, hot day in midsummer.

All of a sudden, behind a bend, a little boy darts out into the road. The driver slams on the brakes. The child collides violently with the hood, rebounds into the air, and lands some ten yards away, at the base of a stone wall at the edge of the road. A truck that flipped over in that same spot a few days earlier left behind some broken bottles. The shards of glass make mincemeat of the little creature, who by now is no longer moving. The blood is pouring from the wounds in his face, head, arms, and legs. Two young girls accompanying the little boy, his cousins, are crying, wondering how they let him elude their grasp. The mother, in a panic, comes running. A passing motorist stops. Together they wrap the little body in a blanket and take him to a clinic in Poitiers. His heart is still beating.

After two days in a coma, wavering between life and death, the boy revives. He sustained a slight fracture of the skull, with a bit of blood entering the fluid in the brain. The other wounds are superficial. Their only lasting effects will be permanent scars, in particular a nasty star-shaped hole in the left cheek, which the doctors say will later turn into a dimple and be attractive to women.

But there were other scars as well. I can still remember perfectly waking up in the hospital room. Everything was white: the curtains, the walls, the bed frame, the dressings around my limbs and on my head. At last I saw my mother, who with tears in her eyes was watching for the slightest sign of consciousness. I emerged from it all without the slightest recollection of what had happened to me. Why was I there? I wondered. My mother told me about the car and the accident. My memory was a blank: no image or recollection of pain remained in my mind. I remembered only the moments preceding the impact and the conversation I had had with my cousins. Then nothing. But this gap aroused my curiosity. I was five years old.

I recovered very quickly. The wounds healed. My dozens of stitches were removed. I was photographed from every angle, in anticipation of the trial, which was held at the court of summary jurisdiction in Poitiers. The driver was charged with reckless driving and speeding. The victim too, however, had been reckless: I had crossed without looking. Moreover, in the court-room I walked with a determined step, and a murmur of satisfaction rose up from the audience: the child would not suffer any aftereffects. The driver was acquitted. This was in 1938.

Two years later there was war and exodus. Bombs fell along the road as we fled the advancing German army. In June 1944, still more bombs fell on Châtellerault, one of which destroyed part of our house; the German soldiers, in disorderly retreat, commandeered my parents' bicycles, though these were quite old. I also remember the unheated classrooms at school, where teachers muffled in overcoats taught us the rudiments of Latin and Greek. I began reading everything I could get my hands on: Balzac and Voltaire, science fiction, the novels of Jules Verne, as well as the municipal library's impressive collection of large, red-and-gold-bound books by a Russian author whose name I forget, in which I passionately followed the heroes in their adventures through the solar system and beyond. In the illustrated magazines whose publication was controlled by the Germans, I followed the stories of the first mail-carrying rockets created by Werner von Braun. Rockets, the sole means of escaping the Earth . . . I also read the books my father left lying about. A certified public accountant in town, he used to tinker with electrical sodium cells on weekends, when the weather prevented him from going fishing; in the evenings he used to read and reread popularized scientific books ranging in subject from physics theories to organic chemistry. I too derived benefit from them, accumulating a self-taught body of knowledge that served to feed my nascent scientific curiosity.

News of the explosion of the atomic bomb, on August 6, 1945, filled me with terror. It also revealed to me that the physicists of atomic structure and radioactivity had been right. I read with great passion, from its very first issue, a review entitled *Atomes, tous les sujets scientifiques d'un nouvel âge* (Atoms: All the Scientific Subjects of a New Age) and all the popular scientific studies of the period. I was about fifteen years old at the time. Was I going to become a physicist? An astrophysicist? A theoretician of matter? Or a chemist? After our house was bombed, the town government of Châtellerault put us up in a rather modern, empty house that had been occupied by the local Gestapo. In the cellar, which no doubt had been used for some sinister purpose, I set up a little chemistry laboratory, where I enthusiastically produced hydrogen gas, sweet-smelling aldehydes, and nitro compounds that had the unfortunate habit of blowing up in my face.

My parents did not look kindly on these childish games. They would have rather seen me study literature, then take up law, to follow in my father's footsteps. At secondary school, I excelled more in literature and the humanities than in math and science. To have a career as a physicist, I would have to get through the university science colleges. I wasn't ready to hit the books and cram for the *baccalauréat* exams required for entry into college. And so I settled for the next best thing: biology. That is, "natural sciences," as they called it at the time, and medicine. I should also add that meanwhile a cancer in the digestive tract brought my grandfather a slow, cruel death. The discovery of this mysterious, inexorable illness no doubt figured significantly in my choice of study.

POITIERS AND THE SORBONNE: INITIATION INTO RESEARCH

After passing my exams before the age of seventeen, I enrolled in the Departments of Medicine—in a preparatory program (PCB, or Physics, Chemistry, and Biology)—and Science at the University of Poitiers. My parents were delighted. They already imagined me as a doctor, well established in the fine town of Châtellerault, living a stone's throw away from their house and ready to come to their rescue in their last days. Unfortunately, I had something entirely different in mind. I wanted only to research and explore the mysteries of nature, life, and our origins.

The Science Department at Poitiers was near the medical school. My plan was to pursue, at the same time, a program of medical studies and a bachelor's degree in "natural sciences." The PCB would allow me access to both. I passed the class at the top of the list—only to learn the next day that a ministerial decree had just changed the rules of the game. Now one needed another diploma to continue science studies! Worst of all, one needed to know the rudiments of geology, of which I was utterly ignorant. Not to worry. With the complicity of a geology professor who was also dean of the science faculty, I spent my vacation that year force-feeding myself in geology, learning to recognize the minerals in the department laboratory. In October I obtained the diploma without difficulty. Both paths were now open to me, and thus I began shuttling between the hospital in the morning and my science courses in the afternoon, returning later in the evening to attend the anatomy lectures of a certain professor Jean Foucault, father of Michel.

The Poitiers faculty offered a very limited number of specializations. In fact, they taught botany, zoology, and geology, mainly for the purpose of training secondary school instructors instead of researchers. Fortunately, in Pierre Gavaudan, who held the chair in botany, I encountered a passionate master of research. With his small team of assistants, he explored still little known avenues of plant physiology and cellular pharmacology.

I myself had begun some modest research in the same areas. With a microscope hooked up to a movie camera, I was able to film infusoria, rotifera, and other creatures inhabiting the local ponds. One phenomenon in particular captured my attention.

One day, while observing a fibrous freshwater alga called meso-carpus, I noticed that all its chlorophyll, which was condensed in the form of a rectangular patch called a chromatophore, turned about an axis in the cellular cylinder depending on the intensity of the light. When the light was strong, the chromatophore would show only its edge. Once the light weakened, however, the alga displayed its full surface. This was one of my first moments of wonder at the numerous regulatory mechanisms that make up the life of cells. This phenomenon had been described more than a half century earlier, but its mechanism remained obscure. With the help of differently colored filters, I showed that it was blue light, not the red light absorbed by the chlorophyll, that triggered this rotation: other pigments were therefore involved. The speeded-up film revealed that the rotation of the chlorophyll patch depended on the movements of the cytoplasm.

This was my first research work. Needless to say, I was very proud of it. The experiment earned me a degree, in 1953, in natural science.

But Poitiers had its limitations. The medical school, at the time, was in fact only a premedical school. The program of studies was only for two years. One had to follow up by going to Tours or Paris. It seemed to me that in the capital the courses in the biological sciences must be more varied, since they were taught by the very cream of French scientists. The physical proximity between the Sorbonne, where the science courses were held, and the medical school would allow me, I thought, to pursue my medical studies and science degree at the same time. I thus decided to go "up" to Paris.

The sheer volume of medical students was so great that, to have access to patients, one had to pass two competitive exams: first the nonresidency test, then the residency test. I thus began attending the preparatory lectures for nonresidency, grumbling and stumbling over the "questions" I had to learn by heart.

I had an excellent memory, yet my allergy to competitions quickly reappeared—especially since the defense of my little thesis at Poitiers entailed significant bibliographical research in a different subject: the L forms of bacteria.[1]

There was no way I could simultaneously carry on this exciting exploration—which among other things brought me for the first time to the library of the Pasteur Institute, the Mecca of microbiology—and frequent the nonresidency lectures, which were becoming more and more demanding. In my poorly heated room on rue Tournefort, the papers on algae and L forms were starting to win out over the mimeographs of anatomy and pathology. What had to happen, happened. I abandoned the nonresidency lectures and the hallowed path of medicine in order to conclude quickly my double thesis, which I went to Poitiers to defend. I then began attending courses in general physiology at the Sorbonne, all the while continuing my training at the hospital in the morning, cutting the medical courses in the afternoon, and then catching up by devouring the mimeographs later on.

I learned a great deal in my hospital training, even though it involved very little direct contact with patients. The Sorbonne, on the other hand, profoundly disappointed me. The courses were usually poorly conceived. Even though biology at the time was being totally revolutionized in the United States and England, the university mandarins pretended to know nothing about this. (The Sorbonne at the time clung to outdated notions and to the cult of the great national prophets of the early century.) Indeed, French research had suffered greatly from the four years of isolation brought by the Second World War. Living science is a community activity. Without exchange, it dies. I had a special passion for the physiology of the nervous system. I read and reread the French translations of English writings on the subject. Nevertheless, one must live. The following year, I stumbled into a position as tutorials monitor for this same certificate of general physiology. When in Paris to deliver a lecture at a conference, Pierre Gavaudan introduced me to one of these famous professors, who was in fact looking for an assistant.

Thus at age twenty-three, I became an Assistant in Cellular Biology at a laboratory of the Curie Institute, an institute specializing in cancer research and treatment, in Paris. A prestigious center for cancer research, the physics section had hosted the two generations of Curies themselves, and the Radiobiology Department had close ties with the Pasteur Institute. My own department was also connected with the Pasteur Institute as well as with the University, but due to a disagreement among the supervisors, we had no ties with other laboratories, despite the passageways between the buildings.

My orientation changed radically at this time. I turned from botany to animal cells and the foot-and-mouth disease virus. In our small laboratory, I familiarized myself with methods dating from before the war, especially the culture of chicken embryo fragments, the favorites of Aléxis Carrel. Then I turned to the suspended culture of mouse spleen lymphocytes. A miserable failure! With good reason: we still did not have adequate growth factors—interleukins—at our disposal, since these weren't discovered for another twenty years. As for foot-and-mouth disease, I was assigned to filming the foot-and-mouth vaccination experiments conducted first in the slaughterhouses of Ivry, then in a fort on the isle of Aix. Though my talents as a filmmaker contributed greatly to my involvement, these experiments too were failures.

Meanwhile, the first rumblings of molecular biology were beginning to reach our laboratory. I had passionate discussions with my assistant and colleague, Jean Leclerc. We were also attending the seminars of the molecular biology club organized by Jacques Monod and François Jacob at the nearby Institute of Physico-Chemical Biology. Every evening I would go to Pierre Langlois's *cinémathèque;* I only had to cross the street.

Nineteen fifty-seven was a decisive year for me, determining my vocation as a virologist. Viruses were then known to have two main components: a nucleic acid (RNA or DNA) and proteins. Two teams—one American, headed by H. Fraenkel-Conrat, and one German, that of A. Gierer and G. Schramm—showed independently that for the tobacco mosaic virus the ribonucleic acid alone was sufficient to allow reproduction of the virus in infected leaves. The proteins had no role, other than protecting the viral RNA against destructive plant enzymes.

After discovery of "transforming" deoxyribonucleic acid (DNA) by Oswald Avery and elucidation of the double-helix structure of DNA by James Watson and Francis Crick, this was the first demonstration that ribonucleic acid (RNA) also carried important genetic information. The fundamental dogma of molecular biology was beginning to take shape: we knew by then that all genetic information necessary to the synthesis of proteins was contained in the nucleic acids—DNA for cells, RNA for certain viruses. Shortly thereafter, the RNA for a human virus, poliomyelitis, proved equally infectious to culture cells. (The beginning sections of Chapter 3 will describe in greater detail what viruses are and how they work.)

Together with Jean Leclerc, I feverishly endeavored to extract RNA from the virus we had ready at hand, the foot-and-mouth virus, or more precisely, from the tissues infected with this virus. And this is exactly what led me to develop an original technique for increasing the penetration of RNA into the cells. It was my first and last research success of the 1950s. My rapport with my supervisor was deteriorating. Viruses seemed to me the simplest of genetic elements; their secrets should therefore be easier to discover and perhaps be of some help in understanding the more complex systems—cells—whose obligatory parasites they were. The laboratory did not offer the modern techniques I needed in order to move ahead. I had to leave.

All I had to do, in fact, was knock on the neighboring door, that of Philippe Vigier, who at the time was (already!) working on a retrovirus, the Rous sarcoma virus, which produces cancer in chickens. He introduced me to the director of the Biology Department of the Curie Institute, Raymond Latarjet, who greeted me warmly. How to guarantee my "rescue"? The possibilities were limited. My future at the university was blocked. I had completed my studies in Science and Medicine, but I had no thesis in Medicine.

I was counting on making my research on the RNA of the foot-and-mouth virus the subject of my medical thesis. One professor of Medicine, asked to preside over my jury, was a friend of my former supervisor. When learning of my inclination to leave, the supervisor became infuriated and asked the professor of Medicine not to preside over my thesis jury. The professor respected his friend's wishes. Such were the mandarin-like customs of French higher learning in those days. And such they still are today, at times.

Fortunately, there were some exceptions. Latarjet found a new president for my jury in the person of a rather nonconformist professor of medicine named Raoul Kourilsky, who understood the problem at once and gave me his approval. But the months were passing, meanwhile. It was already the end of the 1959 academic year. I would have to wait until the November session to defend my thesis. It became clear to me that I had to leave France at once, learn modern virological techniques abroad, and at the same time find a stable situation before leaving. I applied for a post at the CNRS (National Center for Scientific Research) and was accepted; I was awarded a scholarship in an exchange program between the CNRS and the British Medical Research Council, and sent to work in the laboratory of Kingsley Sanders, near London.

These were favorable circumstances for me. The CNRS, an organization founded as a kind of counterweight to the university mandarinate, was enjoying renewed favor in the eyes of the incoming government. General de Gaulle's prime minister, Michel Debré, spurred by his father, Robert Debré, and the few molecular biologists in France who mattered, had understood that they had to play the scientific development card in a decisive manner, creating research positions and new institutes and sending young people abroad to study. This was the time of the creation of the General Delegation of Scientific Research, precursor to France's Ministry of Research.

Thus I was able to spend more than three years in a British laboratory, thanks to a succession of scholarships. I was, in any case, an exception: most of the scholarships were given for stays at U.S. laboratories. In that early summer of 1960, the horizon seemed to brighten a little. There was only one little problem, a small detail: I didn't speak a word of English. I could read, of course, or rather, I could decipher the English I read in scientific reviews. But that was a far cry from speaking!

A British Period

My sojourn was to begin with English lessons at a summer school in Bournemouth. One fine morning in July 1960, I boarded the Dieppe–New Haven ferry with my little car. Once on board, I was already in another world. The coaches of the Paris–Dieppe train were unloading ruddy-faced British passengers on their way back from the beaches of the Côte d'Azur, who rushed forward in disciplined batallions to seize the wooden deck chairs, which they unfolded on the ship's deck, to enjoy a little more of a sun so rare on the other side of the Channel. Once on land, I discovered an exotic country ruled by wind and rain, by tea so strong you had to drown it in milk, and by naturally amiable and helpful natives.

A few weeks later, armed with a few rudiments of the lan-

guage of Shakespeare and a lady friend who was soon to become my wife, I introduced myself to my future supervisor at
his Carshalton Laboratory, in the south London suburbs. I had
prepared a few English phrases in advance. What a surprise
when I heard him answer me in perfect French! Sanders was
not your typical Englishman. A Gitanes smoker and black coffee drinker, he also composed operas in his spare time. Along
the way he headed a laboratory that at the time was one of the
best in virology. It was specifically studying the multiplication
of a little virus containing RNA: the mouse encephalomyocarditis virus, which was very harmful to the animal (killing
it in forty-eight hours) but of no danger whatsoever to humans.

It was no accident that I ended up at this lab. It had already
welcomed numerous French researchers among its number,
and the Sanders family regularly spent their vacations in France.
A perfect, cordial understanding reigned. The atmosphere at
the lab was quite relaxed. Kingsley, who lived north of London,
took an hour and a half to get to the lab each day. He would arrive around 10:00 A.M. in his little VW bug. At eleven the
whole lab would rush to the cafeteria to gulp down the traditional late-morning tea with milk. They were there again at
1:00 P.M., this time for an unvarying lunch, which usually consisted of some meat accompanied by overboiled potatoes followed by a pudding moistened with some custard. Then, at 4
P.M., another tea with milk. At five, laboratory life ceased. Despite this very relaxed rhythm, the research progressed. And
there were passionate discussions, too, with Sanders and his assistant, Alberto Visozo, an anti-Franco Spaniard who by now
knew all the secrets of English slang and was happy to teach
them to me.

While working with Kingsley I became fascinated with the
question, how does the RNA molecule replicate itself? It took

me three years—three years of hard work, Saturdays and Sundays included—to show that, during the reproduction of a virus inside a cell, the RNA also takes the form of a double helix very similar to, though much more rigid than, the famous DNA double helix discovered by Watson and Crick.[2] Paradoxically, this scientific success, which boosted my confidence in my abilities as a researcher, resulted in the dissolution of the laboratory where I was working. Indeed, Sanders was offered and accepted an important post at the Memorial Sloan-Kettering Cancer Center in New York. The researchers of our team scattered, some to the United States, others to various parts of the United Kingdom.

As for me, I had my eyes on California. In particular, I wanted to work in the laboratory of Renato Dulbecco, who was studying viruses as the source of cancers in animals.[3] These were rich times for biological research. New institutes were sprouting up like mushrooms. And British virology, unlike the French, boasted numerous important teams, such as that of Michael Stoker and Ian MacPherson in Glasgow, where Renato in the end decided to spend a year on sabbatical. So much for California! My wife and I were off to Glasgow in our little blue car.

Glasgow, at the time, had all the characteristics of a nineteenth-century industrial city in decline: mine shafts in the middle of town, and abandoned houses where screeching birds took refuge after dark. Saturday nights, beer and whiskey flowed in abundance in the pubs. The Institute of Virology at the University of Glasgow, was a haven of modernity and warmth for us foreign trainees—especially as our rooms were teeth-chatteringly cold, poorly heated as they were by gas stoves in which one had to deposit a shilling every half hour to keep them running!

My greatest problem, however, was an administrative one.

The CNRS would only let me stay abroad for three years, and I had already entered my fourth year. Latarjet assigned me to a fictional laboratory in Paris. Officially I was in Paris, while in fact I was a kind of stowaway in Glasgow. But this was the moment that the science committee of the CNRS chose to award me a bronze medal for work on double-helix RNA. Just my luck! The medal was sent to the Curie Institute and then returned to sender with the message "no longer at the address indicated." Confusion. Madame Plin, chief administrator of the CNRS and much feared by the researchers, was in a tizzy. Latarjet mustered up some embarrassed explanations: "Montagnier? Oh yes, he's training in Scotland, you know, way up there, north of England? But he'll be back . . ." But what was Montagnier doing in Glasgow? He wasn't wasting his time . . .

While I was still at Carshalton, Sanders had obtained the BHK line of hamster cells from Michael Stoker and Ian MacPherson, transformed (made cancerous) by the mouse polyoma virus. He wanted to adapt these cells to grow in suspension inside the hamster's (abdominal cavity), so as to produce great quantities without culture. Kingsley had also learned from another virologist, Peter Wildy, that BHK cells could live at the bottom of a tube of agar. He showed me whole colonies produced by these cells in petri dishes containing a nutritive medium gelled by agar. He thought it was due to some unique property of the cells he had adapted to the hamster peritoneum. During the final months of my stay at Carshalton, I also tried my hand at this technique. I proudly showed Kingsley that a variant of BHK cells which became spontaneously cancerous could also grow in agar.

Upon my arrival in Glasgow, I spoke to my hosts about this new technique. Why not use it to detect cells that have been newly transformed by the polyoma virus? It would be a precise way to measure this transformation which was equivalent to the capacity of forming tumors in animals. By mistake, I lowered the concentration of agar to the very limit, to form a gel. Then I left for Paris, as Latarjet had informed me of the medal business. A week later, on my return to Glasgow, I looked at the petri dishes. Wonder of wonders! The dishes with hamster cells that had been infected by the polyoma virus displayed magnificent colonies of cancer cells growing three-dimensionally in the agar. I announced the news to MacPherson, who calmly told me that he too, using my technique, had obtained the same results. We decided to put both our names on two publications, one in French and the other in English. It is the latter that is always cited.

For the first time we had a precise test, *in vitro* (that is, growing in a test tube), showing the carcinogenic power of a virus. The immediate application was to demonstrate that DNA extracted from the polyoma virus, in all its molecular forms, was equally capable of transforming cells into a cancerous state. This firmly proved that all the information required to cause cancer was found in the DNA. The variant of hamster cells I had isolated at Carshalton, which also grew in agar, was the exception that proved the rule: that was a case of spontaneous transformation, since those cells were capable of forming tumors in the hamster.

A Growing Interest in Carcinogenic Viruses of Birds

But it was time to go back to Paris. It was spring of 1964 and I was anxious to continue working on the molecular biology of viruses, to attack a retrovirus, the Rous sarcoma virus, with Philippe Vigier, and then to apply the famous agar technique to the detection of carcinogenic viruses in humans. If such viruses existed, they should, in my opinion, be able to bring about the cancerous transformation of human cells, such as embryonic skin cells, and this could be detected by the formation of colonies in agar. This was skipping some steps, it is true, since normal cells go through several stages in their evolution toward a cancerous state, and the growth in agar corresponds to a late stage. Normal human tissues, unlike those of rodents, do not easily generate cells that spontaneously skip a primary stage. Nevertheless, I had all the enthusiasm of a neophyte, and with the teams of Philippe and André Boué, I showed that the Rous retrovirus could also transform human cells and make them grow in a very pure agar without any of the negatively charged polymers normally present in ordinary agar.

Quarters were tight: at the Pasteur Pavilion of the Curie Institute, I had only one room and a corridor transformed into an office. For virus detection in human tumors, I was given a little room on the sixth floor of the hospital, across the street from the institute. The experiment was a failure. The human tumor cells, not adapted to *in vitro* culture, refused to grow.

On the other hand, by 1965 things were progressing rapidly with the carcinogenic animal viruses. As for the polyoma virus, I showed, together with Robert Cramer and Raymond Latarjet, that by using ultraviolet and gamma radiation the carcinogenic and infectious abilities of the virus could be separated from each other. The carcinogenic feature was more resistant to radiation. This meant that there existed a cancer "gene" that was a smaller target than the sum of all the genes needed for the replication of the virus. On the subject of retroviruses, we were getting some stiff competition from American teams. Peter Duesberg and William Robinson at Berkeley were the first to isolate the RNA intact from the Rous sarcoma virus; together with Jacques Harel and Joseph Huppert, we obtained the same results a few weeks later.

There still remained the mystery of the replication of this large-sized RNA, whose structure was actually made up of subunits, a fact we were to demonstrate in 1969, at almost the same time as Peter Duesberg. Howard Temin firmly maintained, though without convincing proof, that there was an intermediary DNA (DNA existing during an intermediate stage) in the RNA replication process. I was inclined to believe that this RNA replicated itself like other viral RNAs, by forming a double helix of RNA. In the case of the Rous virus, however, the RNA was not infectious. Sophisticated molecular biology techniques were thus necessary to separate these double helices, notably by using the resistance to the enzyme ribonuclease, which can only digest RNA in single strands.

I isolated just such a specimen of RNA from chicken cells transformed by the Rous virus, but I found the same thing in the control cells not infected by the virus. These molecules were therefore not specific to the virus; they reflected a purely cellular process. I thus spent several years with Louise Harel (Jacques Harel's wife) analyzing the nature of these double helices, wondering whether they might not reflect the self-replication of some of the cell's messenger RNA, the RNA that is synthesized from DNA and then translated into proteins. More likely they were the result of simultaneous transcription of two strands of the DNA double helix of the chromosomes or of the mitochondria. (Mitochondria are organelles within each cell that serve as its "energy battery.") In any case, the double helices had nothing to do with the retrovirus.

That left the hypothesis of an intermediary DNA. We could find no DNA in the viral particles, only RNA. There must therefore have been a specific enzyme capable of making a DNA copy of the viral RNA in the infected cells. An army of researchers and technicians working for the National Institutes of Health (NIH) in the United States were preparing liters of reagents and milligrams of chicken, mouse, and cat retroviruses. This was one of the offshoots of the U.S. effort, launched at President Richard Nixon's initiative, to prove the viral origin of cancer. Underlying this vast program was the simple idea that in humans, leukemias, lymphomas, and sarcomas (three different kinds of cancer) *must,* like their equivalent forms in animals, be caused by retroviruses. To find these, it was therefore *necessary* to start with known animal retroviruses. This resulted in the vast production of retroviruses, which in June 1970 enabled David Baltimore, at the same time as Howard Temin, to quickly isolate reverse transcriptase, the enzyme that transcribes RNA into DNA. For my part, however, still beclouded by my theories of self-replicating RNA, I gave little importance to looking for that enzyme, and thus was left behind by this discovery, which shook up the world of molecular biology.

The discovery of this enzyme, which is present in viral particles, was not, however, the final word on the research into the replication mechanisms of retroviruses. Its activity had been observed *in vitro,* but it remained to be proved whether it would function correctly in infected cells and synthesize a true copy of DNA capable of being integrated into the DNA of the cell's chromosomes and reproducing the virus.

A Czech émigré couple, Hill and Hillova, who had fled the repression following the Prague Spring and had been welcomed by Joseph Huppert in his laboratory at Villejuif, were the first to prove that infected cells contained an infectious DNA capable of reproducing the virus. Their success was clearly the result of patience and tenacity, since the foci (clusters) of transformed cells showing the presence of the virus only appeared after three months of culture! Nevertheless, few people lent credence to their findings.[5] The discovery of reverse transcriptase would, however, have decisive effects on different areas of biology. Most notably, it would make it possible to synthesize DNA from the messenger RNA of any cellular gene and thus open the way to cloning (making exact copies of) genes. Research into retroviruses implicated in human cancers was also to advance by leaps and bounds, since the enzymatic activity of reverse transcriptase made it possible to detect infinitesimal quantities of virus.

Saul Spiegelmann, at Columbia University, and a newcomer to the retrovirus field, Robert Gallo, got into the act in the early 1970s. As for me, I tried to extract the DNA from human tumors and make it enter normal cells, and await the transformation of these cells in agar. In vain, once again! Around this same time I also proposed, at the request of the CNRS, a project for an institute that would bring together the clinic and some research laboratories at Orsay, counterpart to the Curie Institute in Paris. It was rejected.

By now I was itching to move on. Stagnation seemed to be settling in. But where to go? It did not take long to tour all the top institutes in France. Two events then determined the course my future would take. The first was the rise to preeminence of Jacques Monod, who became director of the Pasteur Institute in 1971. The second was meeting the "Pasteurians," among them André Lwoff and François Jacob on the occasion of the First International Conference on Cellular Differentiation in June 1971.

Together with two young colleagues of mine, Patricia Allin and Dmitri Viza, I organized this conference, held at the Hôtel Negresco in Nice, to bring together all the major scientists in the world working in the field of cellular differentiation, the maturation of cells into physiologically and functionally distinct units. We were untroubled by doubt. Indeed, it was clear that, after the molecular mechanisms of regulation in bacteria had been brought to light, the next great question would be whether the same mechanisms also applied to the cells of higher organisms, from sponges to humans. "What is true for the bacterium is also true for the elephant," Monod used to say, but in fact this glib quip aroused skepticism.

Our goal, then, was to bring together scientists who were working on relatively simple systems of differentiation in which the methods of molecular biology could be applied. And one of the subjects discussed was, of course, cancer.

A few months later I met with Monod at the Pasteur Institute. We had chosen November 11, a holiday, for the sake of greater discretion. The head of the Virology Department, Pierre Lépine, was retiring. Ellie Wollman and Monod wanted to reorganize and renew the department in its entirety. There was a building, built after the War, that could be renovated thanks to some private funding. I was a little reluctant to leave my friends at the Curie Institute, to whom I was greatly indebted, and to abandon the field of oncology (cancer research), which was not the Pasteur Institute's specialty. But I was, after all, most interested in cancer viruses, so why hesitate? Furthermore, Monod seemed to me a rather enthusiastic director. I accepted his offer. And thus in 1972, the Viral Oncology Unit was created on the first floor of the virus building. The name made it clear what it was about. However, while still at the Curie Institute, I had begun, with two Belgian colleagues, Edward and Jacqueline De Maeyer, to broach another subject: antiviral defenses.

Studying Interferon

The oncologist's arsenal of chemicals that inhibit the multiplication of viruses is quite limited. Indeed viruses, which are intracellular parasites, actually use to their own advantage the cell's mechanisms for transmitting its genetic messages. It is therefore difficult to find inhibitors capable of impeding viral synthesis without affecting cellular synthesis. Fortunately, all vertebrates have "invented" an early natural defense which goes into action well before the immune system can respond: interferon. Actually, there are many interferons. They are little proteins that today are classified in the family of cytokines, regulatory molecules that cells exchange among themselves. When a cell is infected by a virus, it produces interferon before dying. In still healthy neighboring cells, this protein generates a signal that calls into action a whole battery of enzymes to curb viral multiplication and, to a lesser extent, cellular metabolism. The latter result is the source of interferon's antitumoral effect, which was so well demonstrated by Ion Gresser at Villejuif.

There were at this time a number of excellent laboratories in France working on interferon. The intention was, of course, to use it as a therapy in treating viral illnesses and cancers. Unfortunately, it was very difficult to manufacture. The only attempt to do so, in the 1970s, was made by Finnish scientist Kari Cantell, who for this purpose used white blood cells, byproducts of blood donations of the Finnish Red Cross. Given the difficulties, many laboratories thought to clone the interferon gene in bacteria, in order to produce interferon at less cost. We were among those following this course.

By 1972, together with Edward and Jacqueline De Maeyer, I had isolated interferon's messenger RNA using a biological method. We were just entering the age of genetic engineering. The Pasteur Institute had a relatively prominent place in this field. It took me no time at all to interest Monod in the potential of these techniques for producing antiviral vaccines. An intense discussion followed, at the Pasteur Institute, reflecting the debate that had previously taken place at the international level. Scientists were beginning to ask themselves if it wasn't perhaps dangerous to release bacteria carrying human genes into the world. The newspapers began talking about the "mad scientists of the Pasteur Institute." In 1974, at the conference held in Asilomar, California, scientists decided to have a moratorium. In actual fact, it was very short-lived, and in the United

States remained nothing more than a façade. But we had over-estimated the danger, and those colleagues of mine who were most vehemently against my projects were the first to launch into the field in their own right.

At the Pasteur Institute, a high-security "P3" laboratory (now called BL3 (for Biosafety Level 3) was created to prevent ma-nipulated bacteria from escaping. It was called "the submarine" because it was as difficult to enter as a submarine turret. Four genetic engineering units were set up there. I joined forces with Pierre Tiollais, one of the pioneers in this domain. We needed money, however, a lot of money, to analyze thousands of bacterial clones in order to find the one carrying the inter-feron message amid the multitude of other messages in the cell. It really was like looking for a needle in a haystack.

A pharmaceutical company, Laboratoires Roussel offered us a contract that would bring in the necessary money. Manage-ment, however, said, "Nyet!" Monod had just passed away, and his successors did not possess the same powers of persuasion. The veto came from very high up, from the government, which was afraid that the Pasteur Institute's technological innovations might fall into the hands of the German firm Hoechst, which had just taken over Roussel. They were unaware that the insti-tute did not have a monopoly on this technology, and that it would soon to be used by thousands of laboratories all over the world. In fact it was the Zurich team of Charles Weissmann, one of my former competitors in the field of viral RNA repli-cation, that came up with the first good clone of human inter-feron. And that team included some British and a Japanese, and worked in conjunction with a Swiss-American biotechni-cal company called Biogen. So much for French nationalistic narrow-mindedness! Today the three major types of interferon are cloned, and two of them are industrially produced through genetic engineering.

Applications of interferon are not as wondrous as one might have thought, but they do exist, in AIDS treatment as well. Interferon blocks a late stage in the replication of retroviruses— the retrovirus' emergence from the infected cell. When interferon is present, the viral particles are not well formed and cannot detach themselves from the cell wall. Interferon . . . retrovirus: the connection between the two elements could not be ignored.

THE SEARCH FOR CARCINOGENIC RETROVIRUSES IN HUMANS

The search for retroviruses involved in human cancers was running out of steam. How many times had major journals like *Nature* or *Science* proclaimed "a great discovery" only to see it later fizzle out like a bad firecracker when the isolated retrovirus proved to be a laboratory contaminant, usually a mouse virus! Not the least egregious of these false hopes was the one announced by Robert Gallo in 1977. A human leukemia virus, HTLV, which Gallo believed he had discovered, turned out to be a mix of monkey retroviruses! Indeed, by the late 1970s most labs became discouraged by this sort of research and reoriented themselves to studying oncogenes, genes controlling cellular reproduction and which, when mutated or expressed in untimely fashion, are the source of many cancers.

At first there was the discovery of the *sarc* gene, capable of making chicken cells cancerous. It was identified in the Rous sarcoma retrovirus, thanks to painstaking work in genetics and molecular biology on the part of Peter Duesberg, Peter Vogt, Dominique Staehlin, and Michael Bishop on both sides of the San Francisco Bay.[6] *Sarc* is, in fact, similar to a cellular gene present in the chicken genome, which is also represented in every kind of vertebrate, including humans. It is as though the Rous virus had in some way adopted this cellular gene among its own viral genes, while modifying it slightly. This was the start of a fantastic rush among the laboratories to be the first to isolate the oncogenes of the other carcinogenic viruses, about twenty of which had been identified, and later on, other oncogenes not carried by retroviruses.

My lab did not enter the race. We preferred to hunt for human retroviruses. In fact, a subtle reorientation had taken place, without my even having noticed at first. My interest in nucleic acids, carriers of genetic information, had been waning in favor of the results of this information's expression: proteins. To make an oft-used analogy, nucleic acids are the recording tape or the score for a piece of music, while proteins are the music itself. On with the music!

My research into the mechanism of cancerous transformation had led me, perhaps erroneously, onto a path other than molecular genetics, that of cell membranes and membrane proteins. In the early 1970s, we still knew nothing about the structure of a biological membrane. All we knew was that it was made up of proteins and lipids. But how these lipids were organized among themselves and linked to proteins, that remained a mystery.

The answer was found in 1973 by American scientists S. J. Singer and Garth Nicolson. The mosaic-like structure they proposed explained what was already known, and was quickly embraced by everyone: the membrane is made up of a double layer formed by lipids. This double layer, which constitutes a rather fluid medium, receives the transmembrane proteins, which pass through it from one side to the other. Other proteins, embedded farther out in the membrane and carrying sugar chains, steep in the bath of lipids. The membrane's fluidity explains how the proteins, especially those acting as receptors, can join together. Such aggregations, induced when the molecules attach themselves to these receptors, themselves result in a signal being transmitted within the cell. The presence of cholesterol diminishes the fluidity of the membrane and can thus alter these responses. The discovery of the membrane structure seemed to me as important as Watson and Crick's discovery of the structure of DNA. Yet it went relatively unnoticed, most molecular biologists being concerned only with the central memory, DNA. Living beings, however, cannot live without membranes.

Electron microscopy enabled us to "see" transmembrane proteins, with the two sheets of the lipid membrane laid open like a book. There was a surprise in store for us. The proteins joined together into particles were three to four times more numerous in cancer cells than in normal ones. Buckling down to isolating them and studying their biochemistry was no small task.[7]

The search for human retroviruses well illustrates how dry our work can be. But sometimes when crossing the desert, you arrive at an unexpected oasis. I admit that I stand apart from Robert Gallo on many matters. Nevertheless, we shared one important thing, unbeknownst to either one of us, during the late 1970s: the desperate, despairing search for retroviruses linked to human cancers, in particular, leukemias.

Gallo was not a medical doctor, but rather a biochemist by training. He did not join the "retrovirology club" until after the discovery of reverse transcriptase. His limited experience with viruses at that time perhaps explains his misinterpretations and the contaminations that occurred in his laboratory. But his will and the driving sense of urgency he imparted to his collaborators paid off in the end, and led to the isolation of the human T-cell leukemia virus (HTLV), initially from ill-defined tumors. Later, thanks in part to Japanese contributions (in particular by

Isao Miyochi and Yorio Hinuma) as well as his own efforts, the causal role of this virus in a rare form of leukemia occurring in southern Japan was established.[8]

My approach was a different one. Being well familiar with animal retroviruses (Among other things, I had to cover them in a virology course I taught at the Pasteur Institute), I started by using the animal strains most like human cancers: acute leukemias, sarcomas, and mammary (breast) tumors. The arrival of a new team at my lab, led by Jean-Claude Chermann and specializing in mammalian retroviruses—especially mouse retroviruses, which are quite numerous—enabled us to go further in this direction. Chermann, as well as his assistant, Françoise Sinoussi, and a technician, came from the annex of the Pasteur Institute in Garches (a suburb of Paris), where Louis Pasteur had developed his serums and vaccines and finally passed away.

But the search for retroviruses in human cancers still obsessed me. We had isolated retroviruses that induced cancers and leukemias in all mammals, including primates. Why should man, another primate, be an exception? I knew that interferon was a powerful inhibitor of retroviruses and that the interferon system was particularly effective in humans. That might well be the reason we could not isolate any human retroviruses in man: they were perhaps totally inhibited by the interferon produced by the infected cells. Gresser at Villejuif, and Yves Rivière and Ara Hovanessian in my own lab, had shown that one could increase a viral infection and make it fatal to an animal by injecting this animal with an anti-interferon serum, that is, a serum containing antibodies that neutralized the interferon's protective effect. Sometimes, in a chronic infection, the situation was the reverse. Interferon would become harmful, and one would save the lives of the mice by injecting them with this same anti-interferon serum. At Villejuif, Gresser had two sheep that produced this serum when repeatedly injected with human interferon.

I resolved to try once again to find human retroviruses, this time with the help of this serum. I made the cell cultures, and Françoise Sinoussi looked for reverse transcriptase. The human leukemias we used came from the Cochin Hospital in Paris, from Jean-Paul Lévy's department. Gresser had generously given me a few milliliters of the precious anti-interferon serum produced by his sheep. For their part, Chermann and Sinoussi tried to test my hypothesis in the system of mouse retroviruses. They demonstrated that a mouse anti-interferon serum—also supplied by Gresser—increased the production of retrovirus by the mouse cells by a factor of 10 to 50. We were very enthusiastic about this. A manuscript was sent to *Nature* and was rejected on the basis that the mouse interferon used to produce the antiserum was not pure. This seemed unfair, since at that time nobody could produce enough mouse interferon to make a completely pure antiserum!

As for human retroviruses, the experiments began in 1977. I wrote them down in a red notebook, the same one in which I later described the isolation of the AIDS virus. One experiment followed another, yielding nothing. At times we did observe some enzymatic activity; unfortunately, it corresponded not to retroviruses but mycoplasmas. (See note 1 for a brief description of mycoplasmas, which will be discussed in greater depth in Chapter 7.)

Finally, in 1979 came the big news of the discovery of HTLV-I by Robert Gallo's team. Gallo himself gave a detailed lecture on the virus at Villejuif; HTLV-I seemed specific to humans, but it had been isolated from a rare cancer, mycosis fungoides. There were many skeptics, given Gallo's past blunders. All the same, what held my attention was his announcement of the isolation, by Doris Morgan and Frank Ruscetti in his laboratory, of a new growth factor they called TCGF (T-cell growth factor), which made it possible to culture normal human T lymphocytes over a long period of time. These lymphocytes might be useful in growing human retroviruses, which would be drawn to them. The HTLV-I virus replicated itself easily in these T lymphocytes in the presence of the growth factor, but it transformed them, so that they gradually had less and less need for this factor to become independent and "immortal"— indeed, this corresponded closely with the initial phase of leukemia in humans.

I shared with Robert Gallo the results I had obtained using the anti-interferon serum on mice. A collaboration thus began. Françoise Sinoussi (now Barré-Sinoussi) went into Gallo's laboratory with the mission of transposing the results of the mouse experiment onto the system of a monkey (to get as close as possible to the human model).[9] The point was to see whether the serum would increase the production of a gibbon retrovirus that was chronically infecting some human cells. The results were positive, but the effect was less impressive than with the mouse. Nevertheless, this result prompted me to look for other human retroviruses in cultures of human T lymphocytes with additions of Gallo's TCGF and Gresser's anti-interferon serum. I received from Gallo a bottle containing the culture medium of activated cells including this factor, in an impure state. This enabled me in early 1980 to conduct a number of experiments. But by April 1982 the reagent was used up, and I had to turn to other sources for AIDS viral cultures, which were made in 1983 by Didier Fradellizi at the St. Louis Hospital in Paris.

There was a chance that a retrovirus might be involved not only in leukemia, but also in breast cancer. A good viral model of this cancer existed in mice, which have retroviruses that cause mammary tumors transmitted either by heredity or in the milk. As it happens, in the 1970s a number of researchers, including Saul Spiegelmann, believed they had found similar viral particles in women's milk, especially in that of Parsee women. The Parsees are a very closed Indian sect of Persian origin, where strict endogamy is the rule; that is, they can only marry other Parsees. Now, nearly one-quarter of all Parsee women, even young women, have breast cancer. In North Africa there is a kind of breast cancer, called inflammatory, which also strikes young women and has a swift evolution. Thanks to progress in molecular biology, it became possible to reopen this file with much better chances of success.

No doubt we would have continued down this path if, in early 1982, the search for yet another retrovirus had not become our chief concern. In any case, we had the necessary technology and training to move on from cancer retroviruses to AIDS retroviruses. But fourteen years later, the breast cancer of Parsee women remains a mystery, and even from that distance, my interest in it has not waned.

It was the early 1980s—1983 to be exact. HIV was already growing in my laboratory. I had to abandon all my other research projects since they could hardly move forward while we were refocusing our efforts on the new retrovirus.

Our findings on the retrovirus associated with a breast tumor were nevertheless published in high-level cellular biology journals. They went completely unnoticed. The reader, moreover, would be mistaken to think that all laboratory research necessarily leads to publications of varying degrees of importance and fame. In fact, 90 percent of all experiments lead to nothing whatsoever; most of the time some unforeseen technical snag arises, or the initial idea proves faulty. The day-to-day life of researchers consists mostly of disappointments, with the occasional success that allows them to maintain their enthusiasm. One must have the mentality of a gambler or fisherman. As for me, I am only interested in big fish. But they are rather rare. And so my drawers are full of lab notebooks and beginnings of manuscripts that will never be published, unless of course I send them to *The Journal of Irreproducible Results*.

2

The Red Notebook:
Story of a Discovery

❧ *IT* was in 1982 that AIDS began to capture the attention of researchers. By that time we knew, by the number of reported cases among homosexuals, that we were dealing with a communicable disease. The second group to be struck by the illness, drug addicts, all proved to be intravenous users, and were contaminated through the blood. A number of cases among hemophiliacs also indicated that the infection might be passed through blood products. AIDS could not be caused by a conventional bacterium, a fungus, or protozoan, since these kinds of germs are blocked by the filters through which the blood products necessary to the survival of hemophiliacs are passed. That left only a smaller organism: the agent responsible for AIDS thus could only be a virus.

THE BEGINNINGS OF THE EPIDEMIC

The real history of the disease began a year earlier, over the course of the year 1981. Located in the suburbs of Atlanta, the Centers for Disease Control and Prevention (CDC) is the world's preeminent institution for epidemiologic research bringing together more than four thousand scientists. All health threats are examined with a fine-tooth comb. It is above all in the domain of infectious diseases that the CDC—created in 1942, shortly after the Japanese attack on Pearl Harbor, to control malaria in the war zones—has acquired an international reputation. Thousands of blood and organ specimens and hundreds of viruses and microbes, taken from the world over, are preserved there and used for research. Most importantly, the CDC includes a department made up of doctors and scientists who are "germ hunters" of a sort, ever ready to go anywhere in the world in search of as-yet-unknown infectious agents. In the 1970s the African hemorrhagic fever viruses, which are very contagious, kept the CDC very busy, but by the start of the 1980s the situation throughout the world appeared rather calm.

In spring of 1981, however, the CDC received some curious news. In Los Angeles, a young clinician named Michael Gottlieb believed he was on the trail of a disturbing epidemic: in one hospital in that city, a number of young homosexual men were dying of pneumocystosis, a particularly severe form of pneumonia. Three of them, in addition, showed a decrease in their number of T4 lymphocytes, which protect the human organism against infections.[1] The disease stems from an infection by a protozoan called *Pneumocystis carinii,* a parasite usually easily throttled by the body's immune system. The pneumonia caused by the parasite normally develops only in infants born without an immune system or in patients whose defenses are deliberately suppressed to avoid rejection of a transplanted organ. In Los Angeles, none of the new cases corresponded to these situations.

Pneumocystosis is a parasitic disease so rare that the sole manufacturer of one of the medicines used to cure it never even bothered to go through the procedures necessary to make it readily available for sale. In case of need, one had to go through the CDC, which controlled its distribution. Curiously, over the space of a few weeks, demand for the medicine increased abruptly. This was why, on June 5, 1981, the CDC in their monthly newsletter published an article entitled "Pneumocystosis Cases . . . Los Angeles." But for the moment it seemed of little more interest than the usual litany of food poisonings and fevers recorded from the four corners of the world.

A new alert, however, was sounded a month later. In the July 4, 1981, issue, the same bulletin published a new article, this time entitled "Kaposi's Sarcoma and Pneumocystis Pneumonia among Homosexual Men—New York City and California." It informed the medical community that during the thirty prior months, Kaposi's sarcoma (KS) had been diagnosed in twenty-six young New Yorkers. Dr. Alvin Friedman-Kien was the first to report that he was treating a number of young gay males suffering from this strange and very rare disease, a form of cancer that usually attacks only elderly men of Mediterranean origin. This time the medical community keenly turned its attention to KS, pneumocystosis, and more generally to the infections arising from the destruction of the immune system in gay men.

A task force, under the direction of James Curran, was immediately assigned at the CDC to investigate. Two directions of research were outlined. First, all tissue and blood samples had to be tested to find out whether there was indeed a connection between these different symptoms, as could be supposed. At the same time, as much data as possible concerning the different patients had to be compiled, to find the trail of the disease. Five hundred questions, covering twenty-three pages, were drawn up by the CDC specialists. This was "CDC Protocol 577," which was supposed to give the profile of the disease since, for the moment, nobody could answer the apparently simple question of why these young gay men were suddenly being deprived of their immune systems.

Launched in October 1981, this broad inquiry finally came to an end on December 1 of the same year. All the questionnaires then had to be processed. The number of hypotheses increased, and the pressures too, all focused on minimizing the impact of what seemed to some a veritable epidemic. Nevertheless, the scientific community, at first little concerned by a disease that apparently affected only homosexuals, began to ask themselves questions when other cases were discovered among hemophiliacs treated with blood products.

In late 1982, the CDC decided to give a name to this unidentified illness, which for a while had been called GRID (for gay-related immunodeficiency). It now became AIDS (for acquired immunodeficiency syndrome).

At the time, AIDS was defined as a disease affecting persons under sixty years of age who had no other illness and were not undergoing any treatment that might depress their immune systems. It manifested itself by the presence of one or more so-called opportunistic infections or by the onset of KS. (Opportunistic infections are those occurring only when the immune system is very weak.) By now, the epidemic had already struck 750 people in the United States, about 100 in Western Europe, and an undetermined number in Africa. All were young and showed the same kind of immunodeficiency (a decrease in T_4 lymphocytes), and 75 percent of them were either homosexuals with multiple partners or bisexual. The remaining 25 percent were heterosexual men and women, children, intravenous drug users, recent Haitian immigrants to the United States, and a few hemophiliacs. The profile of the disease was beginning to emerge, but its precise origin remained obscure. It appeared to be caused by a virus. A vast amount of work, however, had already been accomplished in just under two years. We now knew what to look for, and where to look for it.

AIDS Research Comes to the Pasteur Institute

It was at this moment, in autumn of 1982, that Paul Prunet, science director of the Pasteur Institute of Production (IPP), came to see me. He had a little problem.

By agreement, all discoveries made at the Pasteur Institute were exploited by its subsidiary at that time, IPP, which turns over a percentage of its income to the institute. IPP was specifically responsible for manufacturing and marketing vaccines and tests. In developing the vaccine against the hepatitis B virus, IPP used large quantities of plasma from blood donors who were already infected with this virus. In fact, there were not enough donors in France to meet their needs. Thus they had to buy plasma from the United States (2,500 liters in 1981). In the United States, some blood donations are financially remunerated, a practice that tends to attract donors exposed to a wide range of infections, especially drug addicts, who sell their blood in order to buy drugs. In France, on the other hand, blood donation is entirely dependent on charity.

The director of the French National Laboratory of Health, Robert Netter, was formerly involved with the different kinds of viruses that might contaminate the donors' plasma used in the preparation of the hepatitis vaccine. I remember taking part in meetings where the possible specter of a retrovirus was raised. At my suggestion it was decided that a sampling of each batch of plasma would be tested in one of the laboratories of my unit, that of Jean-Claude Chermann, for any reverse transcriptase activity, a sign that a retrovirus is present. Naturally, the test would not be able to detect very small quantities of retrovirus, but it was nevertheless a useful precaution. Thus in the early 1980s, two plasma batches tested positive and were eliminated from the preparation of the vaccine. What retrovirus did they contain? We shall never know, since this hypothetical virus was never cultivated. But this result shows that, well before isolating the AIDS virus, our team and some French authorities were already concerned that pathogenic human retroviruses could exist.

In addition, Prunet felt it necessary to further educate and inform his collaborators by recruiting an immunologist. And so in mid-1982, IPP published an advertisement to this effect. A man who had only to cross the street presented himself: his name was Jacques Leibowitch. He came from Necker Hospital in Paris and had recently moved to Raymond Poincaré Hospital at Garches, right across the street from the IPP premises. He called a new danger to Prunet's attention: that American plasmas could be carrying the AIDS agent. He also told him of his belief that this agent might be a retrovirus. The only known human retrovirus at the time was HTLV (human T-cell leukemia virus), which had just been described by Robert Gallo's team at the NIH.

I did not know Leibowitch at the time. But Prunet came to see me in autumn of 1982 to talk to me about this problem and to ask me if I was ready to determine whether HTLV was present in the preparations he had made for the hepatitis B vaccine. I discussed the problem with Chermann and Barré-Sinoussi, and they immediately accepted the idea of taking part in a research project of this sort. We would have to look for this virus not only in the plasma specimens, but also in the lymphocytes (white blood cells) of persons stricken with AIDS. The task was made easier by the fact that we had used the same kind of analysis in looking for a retrovirus as a factor in breast cancer. We only had to get together with the clinicians in charge of AIDS patients.

There were very few AIDS cases in France at the time, a few dozen at most. Nevertheless—and I was unaware of this at the time—there had formed around Willy Rozenbaum and

Jacques Leibowitch a group of young, active physicians anxious to analyze the disease, assess its development, and distribute information about it around the country. And thus one fine day in December of 1982, I received a phone call from another Françoise, a former student of mine from the virology course I was organizing at the Pasteur Institute, Françoise Brun-Vézinet. Director of the virology laboratory at Claude Bernard Hospital in Paris, she had met Rozenbaum before he joined the Infectious and Tropical Disease Department headed by Marc Gentilini at Pitié-Salpêtrière Hospital. She wanted to bring me a biopsy of a lymph gland taken from a young patient of Rozenbaum to see whether it contained the HTLV virus.

On January 3, 1983, Rozenbaum took the biopsy. He gave half of it to the anatomy-pathology lab of Pitié-Salpêtrière, to have them look for lymphoma,[2] which would have required chemotherapy; the other half was brought to the Pasteur Institute by Brun-Vézinet in a test tube of the patient's blood. As the biopsy was not carried out until late morning, she did not get to my lab until lunch time and had trouble finding anyone to talk to. At last the first two tubes landed in my refrigerator, where I found them around 5 P.M., with a note from Willy Rozenbaum, which I saved: "persistent lymphadenopathy in a homosexual man," it said, and gave the patient's name. He would be called BRU, from the initials of his name.

A New Virus

Why blood? Why lymph nodes? At the time, we knew that AIDS was a disease that destroyed T4 lymphocytes and was preceded by a swelling of some lymph glands (lymph nodes) that could last months, even years. I therefore found it logical to assume that the agent responsible for AIDS existed not only in the blood but in the lymph nodes. Indeed, the latter are, together with the spleen, the body's preeminent reservoir of lymphocytes. Each node acts as a checkpoint against invading germs, viruses, or bacteria. With the subsequent proliferation of lymphocytes, the gland increases in size, and then shrinks when the infection is suppressed. If swelling persists, it is a sign that the infection has become chronic or that the cause of the inflammation lies elsewhere, for example in a cancer. The AIDS task force of Leibowitch and Rozenbaum had also come to the conclusion that a lymph node potentially harboring the virus had to be biopsied (have a tissue sample taken) before the patient began showing signs of immunosuppression: at this early stage, whatever virus they might find would have a greater chance of being the cause of the infection rather than a result.

After dark, having finished teaching my class, I got down to work in the laboratory especially designed to avoid contamination, the nightmare of cell cultivators. The Bunsen burner, long familiar to bacteriologists and virologists, was beginning to be replaced by a new device especially designed for working in a sterile environment: laminar flow hoods. I had only one flow hood at my disposal, and a rather primitive one at that, made of wood.[3] I began to dissociate the biopsy tissue into single cells[4] and after only a few minutes, I obtained an excellent suspension of lymphocytes. I froze one part at $-80°$ centigrade; from this part I would later extract the DNA. The rest I put in a culture flask together with a protein extract taken from staphylococcus and capable of activating the lymphocytes.[5] The point of inducing active cellular multiplication was to "bring out" the retrovirus supposedly existing in a latent state in certain lymphocytes. But which ones? B lymphocytes or T lymphocytes?[6] For the moment, I placed the two flasks labeled BRU 1-3-83 and containing the blood and lymph-node lymphocytes in a warm room kept at $37°C$, ideal for growth.

On January 6, to nourish my cultures, I added some inter-leukin 2 (a growth factor for T lymphocytes),[7] as well as some anti-interferon serum.[8]

Then began a long wait. Every day, I would look at the cul-tures under a microscope. They were multiplying well. Every three days, I would remove a part from the middle of the cul-ture, which I then gave to Françoise Barré-Sinoussi, whose task was to look for the presence of a retrovirus based on reverse transcriptase activity. What kind of retrovirus were we looking for? If it was similar to mouse viruses, the reverse transcriptase would only react in the presence of manganese ions. If it was closer to chicken viruses or HTLV, the element to use was magnesium. We chose to follow both paths.

The blood lymphocyte culture remained negative. On the other hand, on January 15, a small amount of magnesium-sensitive enzymatic activity appeared in the culture of lymph-node cells. On the twenty-third day, a new specimen confirmed the same phenomenon. The hunt for the retrovirus seemed to be producing results. But the cells were beginning to die. If they were infected by HTLV, they should on the contrary be multiplying indefinitely, giving birth to what we call an im-mortal culture of cells. We therefore had to be dealing with a variant of this virus, which infected cells without immortaliz-ing them. In any case, the results were consistent with the por-trait we had drawn of the virus: a virus capable of multiplying in lymph-node cells and possibly killing them in the long run. At this stage, we had to try to spread the virus to other lym-phocytes, in order to characterize it and compare it with Gallo's HTLV virus. I informed my clinician colleagues of these initial results, with some discretion.

If the virus was an HTLV, then it should grow in normal T lymphocytes. I called my colleague André Eyquem, who at the time was director of the transfusion center at the Pasteur In-stitute, and asked him to send me a fresh blood sample. The lymphocytes of the donor, a Spaniard who had volunteered his blood that day, proved to be excellent. We mixed these with what remained of BRU's lymphocytes. After a few days, the culture revived and the virus was spreading again. Could it grow perhaps in the blood of any and all donors? We had no idea! As a precaution, I asked Eyquem to provide me with some more of our Spaniard's blood. Unfortunately, the latter had returned to his country and could not be found. We therefore tried the lymphocytes of some other donors, in particular some newborns.[9] But the virus multiplied without ever transforming the cells. I carefully noted all these results in a red notebook, the same one I had been using since 1977 in my search for retroviruses in human cancers. On the page marked "BRU," I wrote, "at last"—something concrete at last.

Was this virus related to HTLV? To find out, we needed to get our hands on reagents specific to HTLV. It came to my mind to call Gallo, but he could not be reached by telephone. I thought of another solution: to write him a letter and give the letter to Leibowitch, who was leaving for the NIH to meet Gallo and convince him to test the HTLV hypothesis. In this letter I pointed out to Gallo that we had isolated a retrovirus in a patient with a "lymphoproliferative syndrome" without mentioning AIDS; I asked him to send me some HTLV antiserums so I could compare the proteins of the two viruses. This practice of exchange is very common in the scientific community. The use of antibodies specifically raised against a given viral protein is a good method for identifying a virus: it only reacts to the antibody specific to it. If the HTLV reagents yielded nothing, we could be certain that we were indeed looking at a new virus. Gallo rapidly sent us the reagents we had asked for: the antibodies that specifically recognized this virus, and the cells infected with HTLV, which, having arrived unfortunately in a deteriorated state, led us into error. Indeed, Jean-Claude Chermann and his collaborators noticed that the BRU serum recognized the cells producing HTLV: BRU therefore seemed to have been exposed to a virus of this sort. But in fact, this reaction was only due to the poor condition of the cells; it was not observed later, in cells in good condition.

I obtained an entirely different result with one of my faithful associates, Sophie Chamaret: we found that the virus had nothing to do with HTLV, since its internal protein did not react with the antibodies directed against p24, an internal protein of HTLV. Chermann and his associate Marie-Thérèse Nugeyre obtained an identical result using another technique. If the differences between the internal proteins were so striking, it meant the viruses themselves were quite different from each other. All retroviruses, in fact, stem from a common family tree that has branched out over the course of time. Some of their constituent parts vary more than others; this is the case, in general, with viral envelopes. On the other hand, internal proteins are much less subject to change: within a given family of viruses the proteins will possess determinants recognized by the same antibodies.

Our excitement at this point began to grow. It seemed more and more that this new retrovirus might be the cause of AIDS. For a new illness there must be a new agent, we believed. But much still remained to be done. In particular, we had yet to see the virus or to demonstrate that it was indeed associated with AIDS by isolating it in different patients and detecting the antibodies against the virus in their blood.

At my urging, a group was formed which quickly adopted the custom of meeting every Saturday morning in my office to take stock of the work done over the course of the preceding week. Aside from the three Pasteur Institute virologists, the group included Willy Rozenbaum, Françoise Brun-Vézinet and her assistant, Christine Rouzioux, and Jean-Baptiste Brunet. Jean-Claude Gluckman, David Klatzmann and Étienne Vilmer would join us later. New results came in, some faster than others, some more clear-cut than others. The scale was tipping more and more in favor of our hypothesis.

To see the virus, an electron microscope is a necessity. Charles Dauguet was in charge of the electron microscope laboratory of the virology department, and had devoted the last twenty years of his career to studying viruses in the Pasteur Institute lab. He could see them in all shapes and sizes, and knew all their multiple facets. He had also been working closely with me for years. With great patience, working hard for days on end, eyes glued to his microscope, he hunted for a cell—perhaps one in a hundred or one in a thousand—that might harbor the virus. On February 4, 1983, on the cuttings from BRU's lymph node, he found some pear-shaped particles with a very dense, very black core in the middle. These images did not correspond to HTLV. A few days later, on the surface of the lymphocyte culture, he found some budding of immature particles typical of retroviruses. He showed me the photos, some of which were later published. For their part, Barré-Sinoussi and Chermann determined the ideal conditions for detecting reverse transcriptase activity and endeavored to characterize, as best they could, the new retrovirus.

But this was only a first step. To learn more about the properties of this virus, we had to produce it in greater quantity, in lymphocytes from blood donors or in cell lines originating from tumors. All the attempts on the latter, performed with the virus isolated from the patient BRU, failed. That left normal lymphocytes, whose source of blood donors was almost limitless. But might there be in fact "good" and "bad" producers of lymphocytes?

If we were to keep making advances, we would need more personnel and space. In February 1983, I asked the director of the Pasteur Institute for additional space—in particular, a large, vacant tutorial hall located next door to the laboratory where Chermann worked. I was turned down. I was told that if I believed I had found an important virus, I had only to refurbish my own premises! I was, however, offered some funding to buy some minor equipment. Thus was the laundry room of the Chermann lab converted into the "BRU room" for the cultivation of the new virus. Accustomed to working on dangerous viruses, we experienced no contamination during the course of the manipulations. The people working on the virus were, in any case, quite limited in number. I managed to hire a technician free of charge: since he was in a retaining phase, he would still be paid by his old employer (La Française des Parfums) while assigned to the mass production of the virus and its purification. He was put under the supervision of Chermann, who had experience in the purification of mouse retroviruses.

Since the isolation of the virus from BRU's lymph node had been successful, we tried, with the help of Rozenbaum, to redo the procedure on biopsies of patients at the same stage of illness. The results were either negative or created confusion. For example, the second patient, MOI, had antibodies against the BRU virus as well as against the HTLV virus. This patient was in fact infected with both viruses. Gallo, on his own account, probably encountered the same kind of patient, but since he was only looking for HTLV, that was the only virus he found. In a way, we were lucky that BRU, our first patient, was infected only with the virus we isolated.

At the time we were only looking for the virus in the lymphatic stage prior to AIDS, though we also planned to look for it later on in patients with full-blown AIDS. In retrospect, this was a mistake that slowed down the isolation of a strain that ultimately proved easier to cultivate. Indeed, patients with full-blown AIDS have more of the virus in their body, and it can be isolated directly from the lymphocytes of their blood. Moreover, when placed in culture, this virus is more "malignant" killing the lymphocytes rapidly and multiplying in great abundance.

Going Public

The time came to publish our initial findings: the isolation and characterization of a new retrovirus unlike HTLV that grew in T lymphocytes, without immortalizing them, in a patient at a stage prior to AIDS. This patient possessed antibodies to his virus, which eliminated the possibility that the virus might have come from a contamination within the laboratory. This was April 1983, and I was preparing a text for publication in the British journal *Nature*. On Easter Monday, Robert Gallo called my home to tell me he was about to submit for publication in the American journal *Science* his initial findings on the role of HTLV in AIDS, which were supported by a similar investigation by Max Essex also submitted for publication in *Science*. Might it be possible, he wondered, for us to present our findings in the same issue? He was convinced we had, like him, found an HTLV virus and that our three articles, if published in the same issue, would lend each other support.

I wrote the article in two days and turned it over to my most experienced associate, Jacqueline Gruest, who was on her way to the United States to visit her daughter and son-in-law, who worked at the NIH in the same building as Gallo. The manuscript was intended for the editor of *Science* but went straight into Gallo's hands. This unusual procedure was intended to save time, since I had no doubt that Gallo would be one of the experts chosen by the journal for the peer review of the article.

In my haste, I forgot to write the summary that was to be published at the head of the article. Gallo offered to write it for me. I accepted, just to save time. His summary, however, implied that our virus should be included in the family of HTLV viruses, whereas the rest of the article, as well as its title, indicated the contrary. Indeed, we were already engaged, without our knowing it, in a scientific quarrel that would not be settled for a number of years. On May 20, 1983, the three articles appeared in *Science*.

Three days earlier, I had organized a seminar on AIDS retroviruses at the Pasteur Institute. Françoise Barré-Sinoussi presented our findings. Being prudent, we only put forth a hypothesis: the virus whose characteristics we were presenting *might* be the AIDS agent. But we were also proud of ourselves, and certain that our Pasteur colleagues would welcome our findings with enthusiasm. Their reaction was clearly colder than that. It's "the Montagnier gang" crowing again! said some. Why bother working on a homosexual disease? said others. It would put the institute in a bad light and might even threaten to undermine its financing, which consisted in part of private donations.

The international scientific community, upon reading our article in *Science,* was lukewarm. Aboard the HTLV train, our virus went unnoticed. Max Essex's findings showed that 30 percent of all patients stricken with AIDS have antibodies to the surface proteins of the cells infected by HTLV. Similarly, Gallo's article noted molecular signs of the presence of HTLV in AIDS patients, including those of Jacques Leibowitch. In the first instance, the findings were based on an artifact, the same one encountered by Chermann with HTLV-infected cells; in the second, the patients were undoubtedly infected by both HTLV and our virus, but the methodology employed did not make it possible to differentiate the latter.

Despite this disappointment, we were convinced we were on the right track, and decided—Françoise Barré-Sinoussi, Jean-Claude Chermann, and I—to devote more time to this virus.

To this end, we each cut back our research in other areas. We had to determine whether the virus we had isolated was indeed present in all AIDS patients and in all patients with chronic lymphadenopathy syndrome (persistent swollen glands). Cultivating it in large quantities would also make it possible to develop a diagnostic test.

On June 9, Willy Rozenbaum sent us a lymph-node biopsy and blood sample taken from an AIDS patient, a young French gay male whose initials were LAI. His lymph node was invaded by Kaposi's sarcoma cancer cells. I put some lymphocytes and cancer cells in a culture. The latter did not produce any virus. After the fifth day, however, the lymphocytes showed significant reverse transcriptase activity, whereas for BRU we had had to wait twenty-three days. When cultivated onto lymphocytes from normal blood donors, the virus derived from LAI's lymphocytes would multiply very quickly. It would become famous in fact, since this strain was to be used the world over for making blood tests for HIV antibodies. Other isolates of virus would soon be added to this one.

It was time to christen the virus. For the sake of prudence, I proposed two names. We had proof that "our" virus was indeed associated with AIDS and chronic lymphadenopathy syndrome, but we still needed a few more elements before we could claim it as the causal agent. We could therefore call the viruses isolated in patients suffering from swollen lymph nodes "LAV" (lymphadenopathy associated virus), and those isolated in patients suffering from full-blown AIDS "IDAV" (immune deficiency associated virus). Everything, however, seemed to indicate that these two viruses were the same, except perhaps for the degree of virulence. Epidemiological data available at the time indicated that not all patients suffering from chronic lymph-node syndrome would develop AIDS. Even by 1985, we still did not have sufficient perspective on the disease, and we knew that only 10 percent of the patients with adenopathies would develop AIDS within five years. It was thus logical to think that these viruses might have varying degrees of virulence. Today we know that the different strains of HIV isolated from AIDS patients (people showing symptoms of the disease) are more "deadly" than those present in HIV-positive patients (people with antibodies to HIV but without symptoms). But seropositivity (being HIV-positive) almost always develops into AIDS: between the glandular syndrome that precedes AIDS and the actual disease lies only time. We are therefore dealing not with two types of virus but only one, which evolves into a more virulent form through a process of mutation and selection.

At that point, we knew that the virus replicated itself in T lymphocytes, but it remained to be determined whether it multiplied in T4 cells (the the subset of T lymphocytes most affected by AIDS) or in other populations of lymphocytes. To find out, a collaboration with immunologists was necessary. The Pasteur Institute has many talented immunologists. Most, however, are interested only in fundamental problems and work on mice: humans are too "complicated," and the research we wanted to conduct was too "applied" for these researchers, which might seem surprising in an institution founded by Louis Pasteur. On the other hand, Willy Rozenbaum knew two colleagues specializing in clinical immunology at Pitié-Salpêtrière Hospital: Jean-Claude Gluckman and his assistant, David Klatzmann, both members of the AIDS task force. The latter had just learned, in a British laboratory, a technique for separating T4 and T8 lymphocytes. He used it to separate the two types of lymphocytes of HIV-negative blood donors. When each of these fractions was infected with the virus cultured in our laboratory, the results clearly proved that the virus reproduces only in T4 lymphocytes and that it inhibits their multiplication.

In addition, Françoise Brun-Vézinet and Christine Rouzioux were working in Chermann's lab on developing an anti-LAV antibody detection test from the BRU virus produced by the lymphocytes of blood donors. The earliest studies, beginning in June 1983, showed that most patients with swollen lymph nodes had antibodies against LAV but not against HTLV.

One day in June 1983, in the cafeteria of the institute, I discussed our findings, and the virus's very particular morphological appearance under the electron microscope, with Oswald Edlinger, a virologist and colleague at Pasteur. From our conversation it turned out that LAV very closely resembles the infectious equine anemia virus, which is a lentivirus, or "slow virus."[10]

Following our conversation, I raced to the library of the Pasteur Institute. Braving the dust and heat, I found what I was looking for in some obscure veterinary pathology journals tucked away in the attics of the annexes: photographs that resembled the shots of LAV like peas in a pod. Some colleagues at the veterinary school of Maisons-Alfort sent me a sample of the standard strain of the infectious equine anemia virus, as well as samples of serum from infected horses. To our great surprise, these infected horse serums recognized the internal p25 protein of LAV (now called p24), the core protein that is the least variable in the family of each group of retroviruses. I began to wonder if AIDS came from a variant of this virus. But then the horse virus refused to grow in human lymphocytes, and our virus would not grow in horse lymphocytes. Moreover, neither the horse virus nor the Visna sheep virus[11] would attack T4 lymphocytes or cause immunosuppression. They are therefore very distant cousins. But one important fact remained: LAV was closely related to this group of lentiviruses and only distantly related to HTLV.

A Scientific Controversy

In June 1983, I met with Robert Gallo in Paris, at the apartment of a mutual friend, Guy de Thé. Then we had dinner in a fish restaurant on the Left Bank. The discussion quickly heated up. I presented one argument after another. Gallo would have none of them: he maintained that LAV was a variant of HTLV. I believe that at the time he was unfamiliar with lentiviruses and more importantly, that he could not imagine that two so distinct families of retrovirus were capable of attacking humans. However, he invited me to take part in a meeting of a task force he had put together at the NIH, and asked me to bring a specimen of LAV so that his collaborators could analyze it.

And so in early July I was on my way to Gallo's house, located in Bethesda, Maryland, not far from the NIH, with a specimen of LAV frozen in dry ice. It was a Sunday, and it was hot. I briefly joined a game of handball nearing its end in Gallo's garden, once the specimen had been placed in a domestic freezer at -20°C. The next day, the meeting was a festival for HTLV. I was given barely a few minutes to speak about LAV and show the photographs taken with the electron microscope. I made it clear in my report that LAV was very different from HTLV, that it was more like a slow virus, the infectious equine anemia virus. I think only Matthew Gonda, the microscopist working with Gallo, remarked that these images were indeed those of a slow virus and understood the importance of this similarity with animal lentiviruses. The report of the meeting, drawn up by Gallo's secretaries, barely mentions my talk and alludes only in passing to a virus isolated in France, to which he gives the name HTLV-III

Before leaving France, I had had a proposal for collaboration between the NIH and the Pasteur Institute drawn up by Danielle Bernemann, head of the Industrial Property Department of our institute. At her request, we had then immediately deposited our main isolates of virus at the National Collection of Microorganism Cultures (CNCM). I had brought a copy of the collaboration plan with me to Bethesda. However, after the meeting, I was overcome with exasperation that no attention had really been paid to our new virus. Now there was no longer any question of working together on these terms. When I got back to the Pasteur Institute, I was more determined than ever to continue along the path we were on.

Indeed, with the summer came even more proof in our favor. We isolated LAV from the blood of a young hemophiliac stricken with AIDS. He had a brother who was also infected but still in good condition. Both of them, suffering from hemophilia B, had received blood products (factor IX) prepared by the French National Center of Blood Transfusions (CNTS). But during a vacation in Austria, they had also received preparations made with American plasma, and thus the origin of their contamination remained undetermined.

The first epidemiological studies (which seek to determine the prevalence of a disease in a community) were conducted in our laboratory by Françoise Brun-Vézinet and Christine Rouzioux with the help of the very first ELISA (enzyme-linked immunosorbent assay) tests. These showed that most patients suffering from lymphadenopathy had antibodies against the virus LAV and were therefore infected by the same type of virus.[12] In any case, we had enough information to take action and present our case to the authorities and the scientific community.

In August 1983, I sent a series of letters, almost identical in content, to the competent French authorities: the director general of the National Center for Scientific Research (CNRS), the director general of INSERM (National Institute of Medical Re-

search), the director general of Health, and the director of research at the Ministry of Research. In these letters I said:

> Recent findings indicate that a young hemophiliac stricken
> with AIDS has been infected with the LAV [HIV] virus. The
> cause of infection was most probably the antihemophilic
> concentrates he receives regularly. These fragmentary data
> authorize me to consider this virus potentially dangerous to
> humans and to alert the relevant authorities to the national
> benefit that would be gained by very quickly developing the
> means to diagnose and prevent the dissemination of this
> virus, since we cannot exclude the possibility of its spread
> through blood products.

I also wrote to Professor Soulié, director of the CNTS, to inform him of the need to heat antihemophilic products.

These letters received almost nothing more than polite
replies, with the exception of a visit from two colléagues close
to the decision-making process, Jean-Paul Lévy and Jean-
François Bach, and the allocation of 500,000 francs from the
Ministry of Research. This was not enough to construct a P3
[BL3] laboratory, the kind of security laboratory needed to
safely produce the virus in mass quantities.

Why all the fuss over the hundred or so cases of AIDS
recorded in France, the great majority of which were homosexuals? That was not a problem of public health. What's more,
our findings might even not be true, since they were not consistent with the Americans' findings. Only a Charles de Gaulle,
at the political level, or a Jacques Monod, at the scientific level,
could have understood and taken the necessary steps to quickly
expand our research and develop a blood test. But these two
were no longer with us.

As for the specialists, their response was no better. I was invited by Gallo to a colloquium on retroviruses which James

Watson had asked him to organize at Cold Spring Harbor, together with Max Essex and Ludwig Gross, the discoverer of the first mouse leukemia retrovirus. Cold Spring Harbor Laboratory, on Long Island, New York, is the Mecca for molecular biologists: James Watson, one of the "fathers" of the double helix, developed molecular biology laboratories there and made the place into an incomparable conference center. The colloquium focused on HTLV and leukemia: only one session, the last, would deal with AIDS. The date was September 15, 1983.[13] Many of the participants had already left; I spoke to a half-empty hall. Moreover, the chairman of the session, Don Francis of the CDC, seemed anxious to conclude and granted me no grace period beyond the twenty-minute limit. A barrage of questions followed my presentation, some of them honest, some of them less so: Was I really sure it was a retrovirus? Did we really observe reverse transcriptase activity? Guy de Thé himself told me he was convinced we had found a new retrovirus. But he expressed his reservations as to its causal role. As for Gallo, I asked him to explain the reason for his position, while he had all the details of our work in his hands in the form of my manuscript. "You punched me out," he said. That is, I had demolished all his work on HTLV and AIDS. And yet, in the conclusion of my report, in an attempt to be open-minded, I did not rule out HTLV either. I had naively believed I would convince the doubters, whereas I was up against a wall of indifference and bad faith.

Before returning to Paris I gave a speech in New York, at the Rockefeller University. The attendees listened to me politely, nothing more. On my way back, I had planned to give a press conference as well as an interview. The interview was to be conducted by John Maurice, a journalist who had talked about LAV (and HTLV) in the *Journal of the American Medical Association (JAMA)*. I canceled the interview, and the Pasteur Institute management, in agreement with the CNRS, asked me to cancel my press conference scheduled for Paris as well, in lieu of which they published a simple press release. But still another disappointment awaited me. Klatzmann had drafted an article on the virus's tropism for (attraction to) T4 lymphocytes, which he had submitted for publication to *Nature*. The journal turned it down. One of the experts consulted denied the human origin of LAV: was it not a laboratory contaminant originating in a mouse virus? And yet we knew this was impossible, since the patient had antibodies against his own virus. In addition, this expert rather elegantly advised us to wait for two years before publishing our report, "as Robert Gallo would have done for HTLV." No doubt this English consultant was close to HTLV supporters. Despite our protests, our replies, our explanations, there was no appealing this decision, a strangely hostile stance for a high-level scientific journal toward a rather extraordinary discovery.

In anger, I sent to the *Nature* editor a copy of the manuscript I had presented at Cold Spring for publication in the book of the conference, which was supposed to be published in January 1984. In fact I was one of the few to turn in my manuscript before the deadline. The book would not be published until June 1984, and would contain a few chapters on Gallo's new HTLV-III virus (identical to LAV) written in 1984, well after the conference. As for the article on T4 tropism, which was important in proving the role of LAV in AIDS, it was to suffer an even more sinister fate. After it was turned down by *Nature,* Gluckman and Klatzmann rewrote it and sent it to another high-level journal, the American *Proceedings of the National Academy of Science (PNAS)*. The paper first had to be presented to *PNAS* by a member of the academy, who would select two experts to review it. André Lwoff, a renowned Pasteurian, agreed to present the article, and I proposed to him a list of possible experts. One of them never even sent back his opinion, as though he had never received the manuscript, and Lwoff did not dare send it to another expert. Finally, in the spring of 1984, we sent it to *Science.* Gallo's articles on HTLV-III had already appeared, and Ruth Kulstadt, one of the *Science* editors, told us she would be interested in articles by the French group. Klatzmann and Gluckman rewrote it a third time—overnight—and the new version was published in July 1984, almost a year after the initial submission to *Nature!*

Meanwhile, an article I had sent to *Science* on the similarity between LAV and the horse anemia virus did not enjoy a better fate. I finally published it in March 1984 in the annals of the Pasteur Institute. I still retain—and I think the same is true for associates and colleagues—a feeling of bitterness about this period. We knew we were right, but we were the only ones. Many discoverers must have had the same experience, but this time it was a question of public health. I have often wondered if there was any way things could have happened differently. Perhaps we should have immediately published our findings in French-language journals such as *Les Comptes rendus de l'Académie des sciences* (Reviews of the Academy of Sciences) and alerted the press. But I am not entirely convinced. The French virological community was itself resigned to seeing the light come only from across the Atlantic. Even Jacques Leibowitch, so far ahead of the rest in promoting the notion of a retrovirus, never got past HTLV and even as late as March 1984 published a book entitled *Un Virus venu d'ailleurs* (A virus from elsewhere), in which HTLV is presented as the cause of AIDS and LAV is accorded but a single paragraph. As for the press, the newspapers that set the tone, such as *Le Monde,* were leaning toward Robert Gallo, despite having published one of the first articles favorable to the LAV thesis, written by its medical writer Jean-Yves Nau, who was harshly criticized for it. A conference organized in Paris in October 1983 by the Association pour la Recherche sur le Cancer (Association for Cancer Research) (ARC) pitted me against Gallo. I presented the initial results of the ELISA test and announced that the test would be marketed by IPP. My American colleague then stood up to warn IPP and the French authorities against such a venture. It was the same story at a meeting organized by INSERM at Seillac, in the Loire Valley: even French "experts" in electron microscopy cast doubt on the retroviral nature of LAV. I guess it is the fate of pioneers never to be understood right away! But this sort of ignorance—mere stupidity or bad faith?—was to cause delays in developing the detection test, which would have deadly consequences for hemophiliacs and transfusion recipients. Fortunately, a few months later, the wind was to change direction.

Meanwhile findings continued to come in from our laboratory. The initial BRU virus was changing upon serial passages (growth from generation to generation) in lymphocyte cultures. It had become fatal to lymphocytes in culture. In October, with my late lamented colleague Jacqueline Gruest, I discovered a new property of the virus, one that we had looked for in vain upon first isolating it: it multiplied in continuous lines of tumor cells. These were not T_4 lines, but rather antibody-producing cells (B lymphocytes) that had been either immortalized by the Epstein-Barr virus (EBV, an infectious agent of the herpes group) or taken from Burkitt's lymphomas (lymph tumors found in African children). This discovery ensured a better production of virus.

We ascribed these changes to the long stretches of time spent in vitro by the BRU virus. In particular, the Klatzmann-Gluckman group and Chermann had tried to infect some precursors of T lymphocytes present in the bone marrow. The experiment proved inconclusive, but the virus that was propagated in this fashion seemed to have given birth to a livelier, more virulent variant, called MT. It was this MT virus that I used in the experiments with the lines of B lymphocytes. Also, in September 1983, despite the growing mistrust that was beginning to come between us and Robert Gallo, we once again sent him, at his request, two specimens of virus, one of which was MT.[14] The July specimen, by his account, would not grow in his laboratory. We now know—having only found out in 1991—that this MT virus was not BRU's, but came from the patient LAI. Was this due to a labeling error, an accidental mix-up that occurred when the BRU, LAI, and LOI viruses were all grown in culture at the same time for the production of the ELISA test? It is important to understand that when an infectious agent reproduces faster than others, even if it is initially present in a smaller quantity, it can quickly replace the other variants.[15] Whatever the case, the BRU/MT/LAI virus had contaminated the local viral strains of several outside laboratories, including Gallo's in the United States, and that of Robin Weiss, a well-known retrovirus specialist in London.

In February 1984, Chermann and Brun-Vézinet left for Park City, Utah, where one of the multiple conferences organized each winter by UCLA is held. Chermann presented all of our findings on AIDS, while Gallo publicly stuck to his position regarding HTLV. Many things were happening in his laboratory—as we were to find out later. Mika Popovic, a Slovak researcher who had worked on retroviruses at Bratislava, had rejoined Gallo's team. He was the one in charge of all the HTLV-I cultures. In autumn of 1983, he succeeded in making our MT virus grow on lines of T4 tumor cells. He was about to characterize it and notified Robert Gallo of this, but was told to keep silent. When, in December, Popovic called me to ask for some anti-interferon serum, he was careful not to tell me that he had learned how to cultivate our virus on a continuous cell line, and only laconically remarked: "I know how to grow your virus."

Chermann was given a better reception at Park City than I had received at Cold Spring Harbor. The CDC researchers, especially Don Francis, were more open this time and recognized the validity of our work. The research on HTLV was going nowhere, while our work was making progress. The LAV ELISA test, thanks to the virus produced on continuous cell lines, was of a high quality.

In late March of 1984, Robert Gallo telephoned me to say he had isolated a new virus that was growing very well, an HTLV a bit different from the others that he called HTLV-III. In his opinion, it was the AIDS agent. Had he compared it with LAV? I asked. I could not hear the answer. A few days later at the beginning of April, he came to Paris. Chermann had invited him, along with several CDC researchers, including Francis, to give a series of lectures to French scientists on the retroviral origin of AIDS. Gallo refused to talk about HTLV-III in public, as his findings were to be published in *Science* in early May. But in private he agreed to give us a few details. Francis wanted to be present at this meeting. He too had isolated a virus comparable to ours, at the CDC in Atlanta. But Gallo refused to speak about HTLV-III with him present: one more virus is meaningless, compared to his own forty-eight isolates, he said. I was very troubled by this reaction, which was rather discourteous, to say the least. Finally, Francis agreed to leave the room, while the three of us—Chermann, Barré-Sinoussi, and myself—remained with Gallo. The latter repeated that he had not compared his new virus to LAV, but said he was ready to do this in a collaboration whose findings would be made known worldwide. Moreover, his findings would be presented at a press conference, although the time and place of the announcement were no longer his to decide, but the U.S. government's.

We were satisfied, since the HTLV-III virus Gallo described to us resembled LAV/MT like an identical twin. But we were also disappointed, since ethically speaking he ought to have already compared it with the virus we had sent to him, and if identical, should not have changed its name. This is my main criticism of Robert Gallo. He later acknowledged his mistake in private conversations, and believes he has paid dearly for it. Especially as his most famous isolate, HTLV-IIIB—the one which has been used in all American blood detection tests—has proved to be but a contamination of the Pasteur virus LAV/MT2 (in fact, LAI).[16] But let's not get ahead of ourselves . . .

The press conference was held on April 28, 1984 in Washington, D.C. Gallo, sounding very tense, telephoned me before and after the event. I advised him to make sure to mention the work we at Pasteur had done. In fact, the press conference, as it was reported on the teletypes and later over the radio, proclaimed a great victory for American science. The Secretary of the U.S. Department of Health and Human Services, Margaret Heckler, lost her voice at an unfortunate moment, preventing her from reading the paragraph that was supposed to give credit to the work of the Pasteur team. Even after fifteen years these events still leave a bitter taste in my mouth, even though I am aware that the extraordinary publicity Gallo rallied around his virus reflected onto ours. For the entire scientific community, in any case, the cause was now understood: LAV/HTLV-III was indeed the cause of AIDS, period.

DEVELOPING A COMMERCIAL
AIDS BLOOD TEST

For my dear French colleagues, the light had finally come from America. It was about time. For we had to start thinking about practical applications at once. While a few weeks earlier, an LAV detection test for the blood-transfusion centers was deemed too expensive and useless, our industrial partners had now started to mobilize and were asking for our technical assistance.

In the United States the NIH sent out an invitation for bids to the various companies involved in the field, and awarded a liter of HTLV-III-infected cell culture to five important companies with a great deal of experience in diagnostic testing: Abbott Laboratories, Du Pont, Ortho Diagnostics, BioRad Laboratories, and Organon Teknika. In France, on the other hand, no invitation to tender was made, since by agreement our discovery was to be exploited by the industrial subsidiary of the Pasteur Institute, the IPP, which had been split in two companies at the beginning of 1984, the diagnostic part being controlled by Sanofi (Diagnostics Pasteur), while the vaccine production part became associated with Mérieux (Pasteur Mérieux Serums et Vaccins).

Diagnostics Pasteur (DP) was a small enterprise at this time, which made it all the more remarkable that the transfer of technology from our laboratory to commercial production could have been accomplished so fast. Indeed, the DP technicians and engineers were the first to benefit from the P3 [BL3] safety laboratory that I had been requesting for our team since August 1983. In January 1984, the Pasteur management had finally decided to build it using institute funds. It was completed in June of that same year and was used by the DP engineers before they moved viral production to their own laboratory at Garches, a suburb of Paris.

To produce the virus in mass quantities, we also had to take advantage of a line of cells producing a high output of the virus. We could obtain considerable quantities of the virus in the laboratory using lymphocytes from blood donors. In the 1970s This same procedure enabled Kari Cantell to produce interferon en masse in Finland, before genetic engineers learned how to produce it from bacteria. It was therefore possible, for lack of anything better, to adapt this procedure to an industrial scale. But something better came along quickly: by early 1984, we had at our disposal a tumor cell line derived from B lymphocytes that was producing the MT virus without being killed by it. We only had to replenish the culture with new cells from time to time, when the output slackened. Then, thanks to some British collaborators, we used an even better T-cell line called CEM, derived from the leukemic cells of a child with acute lymphoid leukemia.

In September 1983, the European Community began to show interest in AIDS, and a European AIDS task force was created in Brussels. One of its first initiatives was to invite Robert Gallo and myself to present our findings on HTLV-I and LAV, respectively. Many participants seemed convinced about LAV, especially the English representative, David Tyrell, who passed the information on to Robin Weiss.

Robin phoned me to ask if he could send me one of his young associates, Rachanee Cheingsong-Popov, to learn the techniques of growing LAV in lymphocytes. The young woman thus came to my laboratory in February 1984 for her training, and then left with the BRU/MT2 strain. Two months later she returned to my laboratory with a CEM cell line infected by this virus. Since we had already tried the same experiment several months earlier with the freshly isolated BRU strain and had failed, I believed (mistakenly) that the difference was not that our virus had changed, but that Weiss's particular CEM cells must have not been the same as ours. And indeed, when we saw the London strain, it looked particularly rich in virus.

I thus began to propose to Weiss and to the institution he directed, the cancer research laboratories of the Chester-Beatty Institute, that we collaborate on an industrial application of this CEM line. Before transferring it to Diagnostics Pasteur, however, I had it checked to be sure it was devoid of mycoplasmas, which frequently contaminate tumor cell lines. As it turned out, the cell culture was found to be highly contaminated by mycoplasmas and for this reason died very soon after infection. It was therefore unusable at the industrial level.

I decided to turn to the "cell library," the American Type Culture Collection, to go back to the original CEM line as it had been registered in 1965 by its American "inventor" Foley and derived from a child with leukemia. Indeed, it was guaranteed to be without mycoplasmas (and in fact had very minor residual contamination).[17] By April 1984, our ELISA lab tests, manufactured from viruses produced on B-cell lines, were giving the same good response on coded serums sent to us by the CDC as was the ELISA test of the virus produced on Robert Gallo's own H9 cell line.

At that famous meeting with Robert Gallo in early April 1984 in Paris, we had agreed to trade viruses—though rather unenthusiastically. Indeed, remembering what Mika Popovic had said about having found out how to make our virus grow, I thought that Gallo's lab alone should have to make the comparison. All the same, it was decided that an associate of Gallo, Sarngadharan (known as Sarang), would bring us some inactivated "HTLV-III" virus so we could compare its proteins side by side by gel electrophoresis with LAV's proteins and their reactivity to patients' serums. (Gel elechophoresis is a biochemical method of identifying proteins based on their molecular weight.) Sarang arrived May 15, 1984, with some living virus and infected H9 cells, which was not exactly what we had agreed to! And of course the comparison showed that the viruses were closely related. Indeed, as I later found out, they were twins. There were some discussions about how to interpret the surface proteins of the virus. At the time, neither Gallo's team nor my own had yet identified the "large" surface protein of the virus, the one that is so important in detecting antibodies to the virus. This protein, called gp120, was discovered in autumn 1984 by both Max Essex and myself independently. Earlier, using the Western blot technique (which matches antibodies to specific proteins), Gallo and his associates had succeeded in identifying gp41, the "small" protein that serves as the large protein's support. Our own techniques had been unsuccessful in this search, especially as the protein could be easily confused with a cellular protein, actin, carried away by the virus, and with a precursor of the virus's core proteins.

The second comparison was to take place at Bethesda in Gallo's laboratory. The point was to compare the nucleic acids by using what are called restriction patterns: Restriction enzymes are able to cut DNA at specific points defined by short specific nucleotide sequences. The size of the resulting DNA pieces is therefore dependent on the position of the specific cuts. If two DNA sequences are identical, the restriction pattern (the sizes of the DNA pieces) should therefore be the same. But a single nucleotide change in a restriction point could suppress recognition by a restriction enzyme and hence the corresponding cut, giving rise to a larger DNA piece and a different restriction pattern.

In the two respective laboratories, the race to clone the genes of the virus had begun. But Gallo's laboratory, which had greater resources in this area, was more advanced. He had already compared the restriction markers of several isolates of virus and found differences already showing the virus's extreme variability. But what a surprise, the restriction markers of HTLV-III and LAV/BRU were strictly identical!

Around July 1984, Gallo phoned me to tell me this amazing result, while implying that I might have contaminated our LAV with the living virus that Saran had brought to our laboratory in May 1984. Gallo wrote later that I had no reaction to this. If we had used videophones, he would have seen me literally leap out of my chair, on the verge of apoplexy! I retorted that if there had been any contamination, it could only have happened at his end. Indeed, I had sent LAV/MT2 to other laboratories than his—notably to that of Malcom Martin, one of his

colleagues at the NIH, in April 1984—before we had even received Gallo's HTLV-IIIB, and Malcolm also found an identical
restriction pattern in the two viruses.

Around this time, I began seriously to ask myself, like the
young molecular biologists around me, whether HTLV-IIIB
was not merely another name for LAV.

SEQUENCING THE VIRUS

The study of LAV through molecular biology was swiftly progressing in our laboratories, even though it had been so difficult to get off the ground. I had assigned to Marc Alizon, a
young physician doing his military service at Percy Hospital
who had been assigned to my laboratory, the arduous task of
cloning, in bacteria, the DNA synthesized from the viral RNA
through reverse transcriptase. We would then use this DNA as
a probe to pick up the proviral DNA (the initial DNA copy of
The Viral RNA) carrying all the genetic information about the
virus in the infected cells. In a third phase, sequencing would
make it possible to know the 9,000 "sequences" of the four
bases (the four letters of the genetic alphabet) making up the
genetic code of the virus, and to determine how many genes it
contained and how many proteins could be synthesized from
this code. The first phase was realized, not without difficulty,
by Marc Alizon. A more substantial team made up of Pierre
Tiollais, Pierre Sonigo, and Simon Wain-Hobson, came and
joined forces with him to execute the second phase. Finally, for
the third phase, the institute's directors, who were beginning
to grasp the significance of AIDS and the research we were
doing, added two young researchers, Olivier Danos and Stuart
Cole, both "borrowed" from other Pasteur laboratories. These
highly motivated "five musketeers," working night and day,
found the sequence in record time, actually making up all the

time we had lost in falling behind the American teams. And this even though Robert Gallo was surrounded by some twenty researchers, some of them from large pharmaceutical laboratories.[18] In November 1984, in any case, the LAV/BRU/MT2 sequence was completed at Pasteur.

I was invited, with Jean-Claude Chermann, to participate in a congress on the AIDS viruses at the NIH, organized by Sam Broder, then director of the National Cancer Institute (NCI). As Chermann was unavailable, I suggested to Broder that he invite Simon Wain-Hobson in his place, to present LAV's gene structure. There were many surprising things in this structure. Aside from the classic genes present in all retroviruses, Wain-Hobson and his colleagues had identified a whole series of small genes to which they assigned the letters F, Q, R, S, T. These small genes did not exist in known animal retroviruses. Moreover, the sequence of the LAV virus placed it at the entirely opposite end of the retroviral family tree from the HTLV virus, thus confirming its classification as a lentivirus. I sensed that Broder was quite reticent about Wain-Hobson's presentation. In the end I managed to secure for Wain-Hobson the same amount of time to speak as I would be allowed: twenty minutes.

Once I got to Bethesda, I found out the reason for this reticence. The team of the NCI was not quite ready to present the HTLV-III sequence because they were having trouble interpreting it. They wanted at all costs for the genes to be in the same order as in HTLV-I and -II, because they needed the new AIDS virus to belong to the HTLV family. In fact, when Wain-Hobson presented the new LAV genes, the Americans all put on long faces: they had "missed" a gene. At coffee break, Paul Luciw, a molecular biologist from the West Coast, confirmed to me that he had found the same structure as Wain-Hobson in the virus independently isolated by Jay Levy in San Francisco.

Announcing findings at a public conference implies that publication is just around the corner. Wain-Hobson had phoned an assistant editor at *Nature,* Peter Newmark, to ask him if the journal would be interested in publishing our sequence. Newmark had said yes. But after Wain-Hobson returned to Paris, an unpleasant surprise awaited him as he was preparing to send off the manuscript. Newmark no longer wanted the piece: he was only going to publish Gallo's sequence, which he had received first. *Nature*'s editors probably realized that the two sequences would be identical, which would prove to the whole world that the two viruses were the same. Moreover, the rumor was circulating that an emissary for Gallo had gone to London to correct, in the galley proofs, a mistake his group had become aware of after Wain-Hobson's lecture, in the interpretation of the gene structure. We had to find a journal of the caliber of *Nature* willing to publish our sequence at once.

We had our doubts about *Science,* since we knew they favored the San Francisco sequence. That left a third journal, *Cell,* founded by a dissident editor of *Nature,* Benjamin Lewin. It so happened that a friend of Marc Alizon, Pascal Madaule was interning in Richard Axel's laboratory at Columbia University in New York. Axel was a friend of Benjamin Lewin. Some telephone lines between Paris, New York, and Boston were thus kept quite busy for a while. Lewin agreed to publish our sequence in the January issue of *Cell.* I remember how anxiously we watched for each new issue of *Nature,* which appears weekly. Nothing, at first. Then, finally, the third January issue of *Nature* published Gallo's sequence. *Cell* had already come out a few days earlier. There were nineteen signatures to the *Nature* article, and only the five Pasteur's musketeers for the *Cell* article. The two sequences were identical, except for a few errors due to experimental procedures.

Newmark had telephoned me at the beginning of January: he had changed his mind, he said, and *Nature* was now ready to publish our sequence—but in a later issue than the one featuring Gallo's article. I rejected this offer.

Whatever the case, the identical nature of the two sequences was quite troubling. The more likely hypothesis was that the HTLV-IIIB had been contaminated by the LAV, which had been received on two different occasions and grown in the NIH laboratory. The other hypothesis was that the patient BRU and the patient providing the HTLV-IIIB virus had been intimate friends in New York and transmitted the viruses to each other. Today we know that even in this case the two viruses should have been a little more different.[19]

Naming and Classifying HIV and Its Variants

Another cause for dispute between the French and Americans was still the classification and naming of the virus. That the AIDS virus belonged to the lentivirus group was clear to us. Gallo, on the other hand, continued to classify it with the HTLV viruses, to justify calling it HTLV-III.

Science published an article by his group that showed similarities of sequence between HTLV-I, -II, and -III, and then, more curiously, between these and the lentivirus prototype, the Visna sheep virus. The two sets of findings proved entirely false, and nothing from these two articles holds any longer. We were beginning seriously to wonder whether *Science* was not starting to compete with the *Journal of Irreproducible Results!* The Pasteur team, to clear the matter up, also unraveled the Visna virus sequence in record time, using a DNA clone given to them by an American colleague, Hashley Haase. On the one hand, there was no significant homology (similarity) between the Visna and LAV sequences, which, incidentally, put to rest the hazy ideas of an East Berliner, Jacob Segal, who thought the AIDS virus might have been constructed by man from the Visna virus and a bovine virus. On the other hand, the order of the genes was the same, with the same small regulatory genes existing in the Visna virus as in LAV, confirming that the AIDS virus did belong to the family of lentiviruses. In spite of this, Gallo continued to question this connection for some time in several scientific meetings. And yet even his own laboratory had meanwhile demonstrated an important property of the AIDS virus, one that brought it even closer to the Visna virus: the ability to multiply in another type of white blood cells, the macrophages, including the macrophages of the brain.

The Pasteur team of molecular biologists enthusiastically set to the problem of the origin and variability of the virus by identifying the complete sequence of two isolates brought from Zaire. I had become interested in African AIDS very early on. In 1983, a Zairean cardiologist, Kapita Bela, with the help of a team of Belgian and American epidemiologists led by Peter Piot and Jonathan Mann, diagnosed some AIDS cases at Mama Yemo Hospital in Kinshasa. About thirty cases had been diagnosed with the means available, which were primitive. There were as many female patients as male, which proved for the first time the disease's heterosexual transmissibility. Piot had very carefully kept the serums of these patients.

In late 1983, with a reliable LAV antibody test (RIPA) already at our disposal for a number of months, I suggested to him that we blindly look for the presence of LAV antibodies. (His serums had code numbers.) Piot enthusiastically agreed. I gave him the results by telephone: all the patients whose AIDS diagnosis had been based on clinical findings and on the decrease in blood lymphocites tested positive for the *gag* protein of LAV. Piot later told me that it was the biggest thrill of his career as a researcher.

In September 1983 we had also isolated a virus identical to

that of BRU, LOI, and LAI from the blood of a female Zairean hospitalized in Claude Bernard Hospital, ELI, who died eight days later. Her virus is still in our freezers to this day. It was sequenced by the Pasteur team, together with another virus taken from a young Zairean child, MAL. This child, suffering from anemia related to chronic malaria, had been infected with AIDS through blood transfusion and was in the adenopathy stage. His brothers, sisters, and parents were all HIV-negative, which showed that the virus was not transmitted by mosquitoes or other stinging insects, nor by normal everyday contact.

Comparing the two African sequences with BRU was very instructive: the sequences differed from one another with regard to the envelope gene. Not only did they differ significantly from BRU; they differed from one another by about 25 percent. The variability among the African viruses was thus considerably greater than that among the European or North American viruses. This has since been confirmed. Indeed, hundreds of different sequences have been taken from around the world and stored in data banks. Jerry Meyers at Los Alamos has devoted himself to comparing them systematically; he was able to distinguish six, then nine subgroups, most of them in Africa.

But an even more significant variability emerged in my laboratory in autumn of 1985. It was to lead to the discovery of another type of AIDS-related virus, later named HIV-2. A Lisbon microbiologist, Odette Santos-Ferreira, came to my laboratory for a short stay. Together with a clinician, Dr. Jose-Luis Champalimaud, she was studying patients who had all the signs of AIDS but tested negative for LAV/HTLV-III. These patients were all Africans originally from Guinea-Bissau, a former Portuguese colony. When she had arrived, Santos-Ferreira had brought with her some test tubes of blood taken from her patients that same morning, so we could search them for a retrovirus. In the hands of my experienced associate, Denise Guétard, several lymphocyte cultures indeed produced a retrovirus showing the same reverse transcriptase activity as our HIV. These viruses were analyzed in two ways: by their proteins and by their RNA.

The proteins were a little bigger in size than those of the BRU virus, and the core proteins were recognized by the antibodies raised against the BRU core proteins. But the envelope protein was so different in its amino acid sequences that it was not recognized by the antibodies specific to the envelope of the BRU virus. At Claude Bernard Hospital, a patient from Cape Verde had presented the same enigma for years: he had AIDS but tested negative for LAV. Françoise Brun-Vézinet isolated his virus, and it appeared to be of the same type as that of the Lisbon patients. Indeed, if these patients had had antibodies against the core proteins, their test results would have at least been ambiguous. But they had lost these antibodies, which often happens at the advanced stage of AIDS, and had only the antibodies to the viral envelope, which was much different.

The molecular analysis conducted by François Clavel in my laboratory confirmed these facts, and a few months later the virus of ROD (the Claude Bernard patient) was cloned and sequenced in record time by a part of the molecular biology team that had already sequenced the BRU virus.

There remained the task of naming the two types of virus. Robert Gallo had so far refused to withdraw the name HTLV-III, which he had mistakenly given to the first AIDS virus. According to custom, it was up to the discoverers of a virus to give it a name: we had LAV and IDAV first, and it was clear that HTLV-III, LAV, and IDAV were identical.

The affair had become further complicated when Max Essex, a colleague and friend of Gallo, gave the name of HTLV-IV to a virus isolated in otherwise healthy Senegalese prostitutes. Francis Barin, at Tours, France, had observed that these women had more pronounced antibodies to a virus isolated by Ronald Desrosiers and his team at the New England Primate

Center from some macaques suffering from an illness analogous to human AIDS. This monkey virus had been christened STLV-III (S for "simian"), no doubt to please the NIH team. The battle of names came to an abrupt end, however, once the analysis of the molecular sequences was conducted and Essex had to acknowledge that his HTLV-IV was but a contamination of the monkey virus isolated by Desrosiers. But the Senegalese prostitutes were indeed infected with a virus of the same type as our Guinea-Bissau virus.

In 1986 a nomenclature committee was set up, chaired by Harold Varmus, an expert in avian retroviruses and now director of the NIH. The NIH decided in favor of the name HIV, for human immunodeficiency virus. I supported this and obtained authorization from the World Health Organization (WHO) for acceptance of the French translation of the term, VIH. I also christened the Portuguese virus HIV-2, to distinguish it from HIV-1, which covers all the early viruses analogous to BRU. The monkey virus became SIV, for simian immunodeficiency virus. A collaboration between the teams of Ronald Desrosiers and Pierre Tiollais at the Pasteur Institute quickly yielded the sequence of the SIV prototype virus.

For a while Gallo and Essex refused the new nomenclature, but then came out in support of it. At the time, we were in the middle of a court battle between the Pasteur Institute and the NIH. The NIH had taken out patents for HTLV-III which were accepted by the U.S. authorities, while the patent for LAV, although submitted much earlier (in December 1983), had not been granted.[20] A long legal battle ensued between the American and French teams, not to come to an end until March 1987, when a historic agreement was signed by the directors of the NIH and the Pasteur Institute and ratified by Ronald Reagan and Jacques Chirac. The two patents would become the joint property of the two institutions, which would share the royalties.[21]

A history of the respective contributions of the two teams was written by Robert Gallo and myself and published in *Nature*. In the heated discussions that preceded this agreement, many of our colleagues acted as moderators, and in this regard I would like especially to thank Jonas Salk for his help.

There was an equal apportionment of royalties between institutions, but not among the inventors. The three Americans—Robert Gallo, Mika Popovic and Sarang—received $100,000 annually. After 1985, the French scientists received nothing for several years because their royalty share was first used to pay off the legal expenses. Later, in 1991, when the first net positive monies started to come in, the financial share given the French inventors was far from equal to that given our American colleagues.

The knowledge of the sequence of HIV-1 and the discovery of HIV-2 marked, in retrospect, two important stages in AIDS research. The foundations of the necessary virological and molecular understanding were now laid. Strengthened by this experience, we could expand our knowledge to better understand the evolution of the disease. Henceforth, the AIDS teams, including our own, would break down into small groups to work on ever finer points. The study of AIDS has become almost a discipline unto itself. Two important new paths loomed before us: to understand first of all how the virus, by infecting only a few lymphocytes, was able to destroy the whole immune system; and second, to understand better the role of cofactors, mycoplasmas in particular, in the disease's development. We were already leaving the heroic early days and entering a more banal period, one whose history is written from day to day. It is a history built on apparently less spectacular developments. But only apparently.

II

UNDERSTANDING

3

The History of a Disease

IN 1990, the writer and AIDS sufferer Hervé Guibert, in his book *A l'ami qui ne m'a pas sauvé la vie* (To the Friend Who Did Not Save My Life), described the process leading to AIDS this way:

> Before the appearance of AIDS, an inventor of computer games had outlined the progression of AIDS in the blood. On the screen, in this game for adolescents, the bloodstream was a maze in which PacMan, a yellow monster operated by a lever, circulated freely. PacMan devoured everything in its way, emptying the different corridors of their plankton, though threatened in turn by the appearance of an increasing number of even more gluttonous red monsters. If we apply PacMan (a game that took a while to go out of style) to AIDS, then the initial population in the maze would be T4 lymphocytes, and the yellow monsters would be the T8 lymphocytes, which are dogged by the HIV virus, symbolized by the red monsters avidly devouring more and more of the immune system's plankton.[1]

Actually, the situation is decidedly more complex than Guibert could have imagined.

AIDS is viral in origin. Its gravity lies in the fact that the infectious agent causing it is a retrovirus that particularly affects the cells of the body's immune system. A chronic disease, its evolution is usually slow: in slightly more than half the cases, in the absence of treatment, ten years pass between infection and the time when the patient, who until then has shown no clinical symptoms, develops the illness. In the interim, he or she is HIV-positive.

WHAT IS A VIRUS?

In the past, the word "virus" referred to the principle of virulence and was used for all illnesses. When the bacterial origin of many infectious diseases was acknowledged in the late nineteenth century, the words "virus" and "filterable virus" were used for communicable agents that are invisible to the microscope and pass through the porcelain filters that hold back bacteria. This is how the "viral" cause of various plant diseases, and later animal and human illnesses such as flu, polio, and smallpox, was proved. Yet it was not until the 1930s that real progress started to be made in understanding viruses, thanks to the development of cell-culture procedures that made it possible to closely study their multiplication cycles. Later, the invention of the electron microscope made it possible to observe viral particles (virions,) directly.

Are viruses alive? Not exactly, since they only exist as parasites inside cells. Their activity might be compared to that of a cassette containing some information. The device for reading the information—the cassette player—would be the cell. The genetic program of the virus is registered on the tape, which is the viral RNA or DNA. It is hundreds of thousands of times shorter than the tape carrying the vastly complex genetic program of the cell (the genome). To survive outside the cell, a virus is enclosed in a protective coat of proteins (called the capsid), which itself is sometimes surrounded by an envelope of lipids. The capsid, or the envelope, carries proteins whose purpose is to attach the virus to the specific receptor on the surface of the cell. Once this attachment is made, the internal components of the virus pass into the cell, and the RNA or DNA of the virus begins its work. Enzymes specific to the virus cause the cell to produce thousands of copies of the viral messenger RNA. These are like so many messages directing the synthesis of the viral proteins, which in turn form new virions that will leave the cell either through its lysis (by causing the cell to disintegrate) or by budding at the cell's surface.

Retroviruses, the group to which the AIDS virus belongs, are enveloped viruses that measure one ten-thousandth of a millimeter in size; they have the peculiarity of possessing an RNA that, thanks to a specific enzyme called reverse transcriptase, is transcribed into a DNA copy inside the cell. It is this copy that manages to integrate itself into the long ribbons of the cell's DNA that make up the chromosomes. The viral DNA (called a provirus) carries an assortment of genes that are again transcribed by the host's cell machinery into messenger RNAs. These are RNA pieces that trigger the synthesis of the various viral proteins, which come together to form new virions that will bud on the cell's surface. The cycle may then start over again.

The phase of integrating the provirus into the cell's chromosomes can be "silent": the tape of the virus may not be read, and the cell may divide while passing on the viral genes to its offspring. However, the insertion of viral genes may alter the reading of nearby cellular genes on the same chromosome. This is how retroviruses modify the cell and make it cancerous. Many animal retroviruses are the source of different forms of leukemia; some cause mammary (breast) tumors, others sarcomas. In humans, we thus far know of only one retrovirus associated with a rare form of leukemia, HTLV (human T-cell leukemia virus).

Certain retroviruses, however, are not associated with cancer but with slow, degenerative pathologies: they are, for this reason, called slow viruses, lentiviruses, or retrolentiviruses. Their prototype in animals is the Visna virus in sheep, which after a few years of incubation causes pneumonia or degenerative encephalitis (inflammation of the brain) in that animal. The AIDS retrovirus belongs to this group, but like its cousins the monkey viruses (SIV), it has acquired a special affinity for certain components of the immune system: the T4 lymphocytes.

HIV

Particles of HIV are shaped like little spheres, each with roughly eighty little rounded projections shaped like pegs (see the accompanying figure). Each peg contains three or four molecules of a large protein, gp120,[2] which has a strong affinity for the receptors (now called CD4) of T4 lymphocytes. Gp120 is associated with a smaller transmembrane protein called gp41, which, after the virus has attached itself to the cell allows the viral envelope to fuse with the cell membrane, thereby enabling the internal components of the virus to pass into the cell. Most likely this fusion is dependent on a change in the structure of the gp120, a change related to the attachment of one of its parts to another receptor on the surface of the cell.

The internal components of the virus, which penetrate the cell, make up the nucleocapsid. This consists of two identical molecules of RNA and proteins, of which the principal ones are p24 (we called earlier p25), p18, p7, and p9. These internal core proteins are coded by a gene called *gag* and are initially synthesized in the form of a long ribbon that is then cut up by another specific enzyme of the virus, called protease. Also attached to the RNA and ready to work on it when the complex has reached inside the cell is reverse transcriptase, the enzyme characteristic of all retroviruses. Much research has been conducted in the attempt to develop inhibitors specific to these two enzymes, reverse transcriptase and protease.

The organization of the genetic program of HIV is even

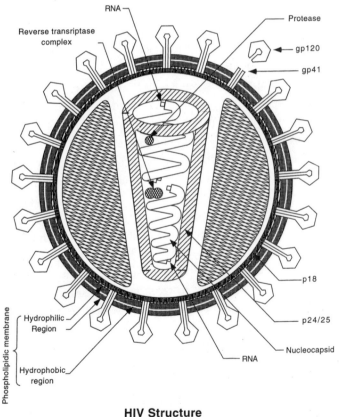

HIV Structure
(According to C. Dauguet and
J.L. Moreau Institut Pasteur)

more complex. At the far ends of the RNA molecule there are sequences regulating the expression of viral genes in multiple ways—depending on some viral proteins synthesized very early, and on cellular proteins present only in activated cells. The activation stage is a preparatory state, when the cell's reproductive machinery is no longer totally at rest but is not yet causing the cell to undergo full multiplication.

Usually, in order for retroviruses to integrate their provirus into the cell's DNA, this DNA must be in the process of replication, and therefore the cell has to be actively multiplying.

HIV does not have such stringent needs; it can integrate its proviral DNA into the chromosomes of the T_4 lymphocytes even when these are not in the process of multiplication. They need merely to be in the activation stage. In the immune system, most lymphocytes, especially those that circulate in the blood, are in a state of total rest. HIV can even penetrate a cell at rest and begin the reverse transcription of its RNA into DNA, but this DNA will not get transported into the nucleus; it dies on the spot. On the other hand, if the lymphocyte is activated, for example by a specific antigen (a molecule the body considers foreign), then transportation and integration of the proviral DNA can take place and its expression into messenger RNA and viral proteins becomes possible. Certain cellular proteins, synthesized only in activated lymphocytes, can themselves activate the mechanism for expressing genes of the virus.

One regulatory gene of the virus, called the *tat* gene, is very important. It codes for a small protein which, by attaching itself to one end of the viral messenger RNAs, will trigger their total synthesis at a very significant rate. The cell will thus synthesize thousands of copies of the viral messengers in its nucleus.

Another regulatory gene, called *rev,* codes for a protein necessary for the transport of certain large viral messenger

RNAs from the nucleus into the cytoplasm, where they will be translated into proteins. These messenger RNAs code for the structural proteins of the virions and also for the reverse transcriptase. In the absence of rev function, only small messenger RNAs coding for regulatory proteins (Tat, Nef, and rev itself) are able to pass from the nucleus into the cytoplasm and therefore are the only ones translated into proteins. It seems that some cells of the brain (astrocytes) are in this situation. They mostly express Nef, which puts them in an activated status and induces the release of factors deleterious for the neurons. Thus dementia, sometimes observed in AIDS patients, may be caused by only this viral protein.

In fact, the most critical regulatory gene for causing HIV disease is *nef.* It codes for a small protein which has many effects, good for the virus, bad for the cell. Normally, CD4 molecules, the main receptors for the virus, are continuously renewed at the cell surface. In cells producing viral particles, the latter can attach to the CD4 surface molecules and reinfect the same cells. This overload of viral infection would otherwise quickly result in premature cell death. But the Nef protein prevents new CD4 molecules from reaching the cell surface, so infected cells can easily release viral particles which can then infect other cells.

Nef has other functions as well. It can activate T4 cells that would normally be in a resting state. This activation, although weak, is sufficient to make the cells new targets for viral infection.

Since the number of activated T cells is a limiting factor for the virus, especially at the beginning of infection, Nef allows the virus to firmly establish itself in the body. Without Nef the virus can still infect an individual, but the viral load will remain so low that it may not cause disease.

There are likewise other accessory genes (*vpr, vif, vpu,* and *vpx*) which have a variety of functions, such as increasing viral multiplication and maintaining the stability of viral particles.

No two HIV viruses are identical. This phenomenon stems from the fact that the enzyme reverse transcriptase makes many mistakes in copying DNA from RNA. Enzymes that copy DNA from DNA are very faithful: they choose the incorrect building blocks (one of the four bases) only one time in a billion. Reverse transcriptase, on the other hand, makes perhaps one mistake in every 10,000 bases. The virus replication cycle is very fast, and the cytoplasm does not have all the bases needed for DNA synthesis in sufficient amount. The enzyme errs because it does not have enough good material at its disposal. This situation might be compared with that of a printer who does not have all the letters of the alphabet in printing a text: not having the letter *a,* he might use *b* instead. What is more, the genetic program of HIV, unlike cellular DNA, has no error-correction system.

Mistakes happen randomly, but only those mutations compatible with the survival of the virus remain. This phenomenon takes place in almost all living beings, but at a much more moderate rate. Thus, when an embryo is formed, almost all the genetic errors affecting growth are eliminated, since they would lead to the premature death of the embryo and to a miscarriage. The genetic diseases that we know are those which are compatible with the survival of the embryo and the infant after birth.

If the reverse transcriptase makes too many mistakes on the *gag* or *pol* genes (which code for core proteins and reverse transcriptase, respectively), the virus cannot exist as such: few mistakes are therefore kept on these two genes. On the other hand, the virus has an "interest" in preserving some mutations in the genes coding for its envelope proteins in order to escape recognition by the immune system. This explains the great variability of the *env* gene. In this sense, HIV is like the *torero* using his *muleta* in front of the bull: each time, it shows the immune system a different pass, thus disorienting it.

All this brings some complex systems into play, some of which we do not understand, but this variability fits in perfectly with the strategy of the virus: to survive as long as possible inside its host. This is why HIV permanently varies within the same person and differs even more from one person to another. This genetic variability is one of the difficulties facing the design of a vaccine, since a vaccine should ideally be effective against all variants. This variability should also be taken into consideration in the diagnostics of HIV infection: the tests have to recognize the greatest possible number of variants of the virus, by detecting the less variable regions of the viral proteins.

The target cells for HIV are mostly the T4 lymphocytes, which carry the CD4 molecule, used by the virus as its primary receptor. Macrophages, which carry the same receptor, are also targets. Macrophages are cells capable of phagocytizing (devouring) foreign particles and presenting the fragments of digestion to the T4 and T8 lymphocytes. When they are not activated, they are called monocytes. Cells derived from macrophages are found in various tissues, including the brain, the skin, and the lymph nodes; they too can be infected by the virus, which explains its presence in numerous tissues and organs.

It is thanks to a second glycoprotein, gp41, that the viral envelope can fuse with the membrane of the target cell. The whole interior of the virus then penetrates the cell, while the envelope glycoprotein remains on the outside. This operation can take barely a few minutes. On a lymphocyte there are roughly 50,000 CD4 receptors to which viral particles can attach. Because of the many errors made at the beginning of infection by reverse transcriptase, many viral "tapes" are incorrect and code for deficient proteins. The result is the production of many defective or incomplete particles. Only one particle out of 10,000 is really viable and infectious. But defective particles, or empty envelopes, can still bind CD4 receptors and cause the premature death of lymphocytes, even though those lymphocytes are not invaded by those particles.

HIV can also infect B lymphocytes *in vitro* if the latter have been previously transformed by an infection from a herpes virus such as EBV.

HIV always replicates itself in the same manner in the cell it infects, following a cycle common to all retroviruses. It is important to know the different stages of this cycle, for they enable us to understand the mechanisms of infection. Most importantly, each stage is a potential target for therapy.

In summary, replication occurs in three stages:

1. The virus penetrates into the cell: the viral envelope binds to the receptor or receptors on the surface of the cell to be infected, the membranes fuse together, and the nucleocapsid enters the cytoplasm;

2. The HIV genome is randomly inserted into the DNA of the host cell: first the viral RNA is transcribed into the DNA of the host cell after the transcription of the viral RNA into DNA by means of reverse transcriptase and then transported into the cell nucleus. There the viral DNA is integrated into the DNA of the cell's chromosomes by means of another enzyme called integrase. This entire process takes the virus only a few hours, if the lymphocyte is in a favorable phase of activation. As mentioned earlier, in the case of HIV, unlike other retroviruses, the cellular DNA only needs to be in *preparation* for replication, not actively replicating. If the lymphocyte returns to a state of rest, the infection cycle can be interrupted and the virus can "sleep" until the next time the cell is activated.

3. New viral particles are expressed (produced) if the cell

is reactivated: the viral DNA integrated into the cell's DNA is transcribed into messenger RNAs, passive carriers of the genetic information, which then leave the nucleus and pass into the cytoplasm. There HIV proteins are synthesized from the messenger RNAs. Finally, viral proteins are assembled which then move toward the surface of the cell to form buds and thus release thousands of new particles ready to infect or bind with other cells.

How to Detect Infection

By February 1983, our laboratory had developed the first test for detecting antibodies against the virus in the blood. Very sensitive and specific, this test (called RIPA, for radio immunoprecipitation assay) is practiced only by specialized research laboratories because it involves the cultivation of HIV-infected cells and the use of radioactive amino acids in labeling viral proteins. RIPA is seldom used today, however, since other techniques, equally reliable and much easier to perform in any kind of biological laboratory, have since been developed.

Several different techniques can be used to detect HIV infection: First, one can look for antibodies secreted by an infected subject. Second, one can detect the virus itself, either as RNA or proviral DNA, or as the specific viral proteins in the circulating blood of the patient.

The most common practice for detecting HIV infection is to look for antibodies in serum and, if necessary, in other bodily fluids (saliva, urine, sperm, vaginal secretions). This approach is used in screening tests as well as in confirmation tests.

In the ELISA (enzyme-linked immunosorbent assay) antibody detection test, each serum sample is incubated in a plastic well coated with whole inactivated virus or selected viral proteins. HIV antibodies present in the serum bind to the coated well and are detected with an anti-human antibody linked to an enzyme. A chemical substrate is added, setting off a reaction with the enzyme that results in color formation, thus revealing the antibodies present in the serum. Many samples can be tested at once in a multiwell plate and the results read automatically.

For screening, it is generally recommended that two different tests be used, such as two ELISA tests from different manufacturers, or a combination of an ELISA and another type of antibody test. If both tests are negative, the subject is considered HIV-negative. If both tests are positive or there is a discrepancy between them, then a Western blot test becomes necessary.

In the Western blot confirmation test for antibodies, the viral proteins are first separated according to size and transferred onto narrow strips of special, absorbent nitrocellulose paper. Each strip is used to test only one serum sample; control samples giving strong positive, weak positive, and negative readings are systematically included for comparison. Antibody binding is measured in a way similar to ELISA with an enzyme-linked anti–human antibody probe that results in a color reaction, visible as stained bands on the nitrocellulose strip. The results are interpreted according to the presence or absence of bands corresponding to certain viral proteins. The Western blot test makes it possible to identify the different viral proteins recognized by the antibodies. The World Health Organization (WHO) has issued precise recommendations for interpreting Western blot tests, and these are used worldwide. A positive result depends on the mandatory presence of antibodies to external glycoproteins gp160 and gp120, as well as to the transmembrane protein gp41 and/or to internal proteins. A complete Western blot profile will show antibodies to gp160, gp120, p66, p55, gp41, p31, p24, and p17.

The ELISA test gives an all-or-nothing answer. The great majority of serums react in an unequivocal manner, above the threshold for positives, below it for negatives. Certain serums, however, are barely above or below the negative control (that is, borderline). A Western blot test will then show what viral proteins are recognized by these antibodies.

When the ELISA test is positive or borderline, and the Western blot shows only one band—not enough to conclude positivity according to the internationally accepted guidelines—then a second blood sample is taken two or three weeks later. If it reacts the same way, without having evolved, or if it tests negative, then the person is definitively classified as HIV-negative. One may speak of this as a "false positive" for the ELISA test. On the other hand, if the infection is recent and progressing, the second test will prove positive. After infection with HIV, the body's immune system needs time to produce antibodies: we call this the "seroconversion time." During this interval, the person is infected but still seronegative, that is, tests negative. Many cases of infection in professionals (hospital staff) show seroconversion between thirty-nine and seventy days after the accident. There is general agreement that the time for seroconversion is around three months. Scientifically, one cannot rule out slower seroconversions, but they would certainly be very rare.

Antigenemia (the presence of viral proteins, hence of virus, in the blood) precedes the appearance of detectable antibodies and is the sign of an infection that may or may not be accompanied by clinical signs. It is temporary and disappears a few weeks after the appearance of antibodies. It reappears episodically over the course of the infection. In testing for antigenemia, a specific ELISA test makes it possible to detect viral protein p24, which circulates in the bloodstream of infected subjects. This technique does not replace isolation of the virus (see below), but in someone infected with HIV, a positive p24 antigenemia associated with a decrease in anti-p24 antibodies seems to indicate a poor prognosis and may help doctors in making rapid therapeutic decisions. Testing for antigens is currently practiced on patients undergoing anti-retroviral treatment, but it is not always positive.

Isolation of the virus is a long and cumbersome procedure reserved for research laboratories equipped with high-security facilities. Most often, lymphocytes from the blood are used, and the culture medium contains growth factors necessary for their multiplication. The cells are then cultivated together with lymphocytes of seronegative (that is, normal uninfected) donors and maintained for some six weeks. One recent technique allows for separation and culture of T4 lymphocytes on their own; as these are the favorite targets of the virus, isolation of the virus is thus made easier. The presence of the virus is detected by the reverse transcriptase activity and the presence of the p24 antigen in the culture medium. This technique is used for early diagnosis of infection in newborns of HIV-positive mothers. In rare instances, it is used to confirm the diagnosis in people who may have been infected but whose serology is difficult to interpret. In this instance new viral strains are isolated which are very distant variants of the prototype strains.

In the test for RNA or proviral DNA through PCR (polymerase chain reaction), a copy of viral DNA or RNA is captured and magnified synthetically up to 100,000 times, thus allowing it to become detectable. Great progress has been made toward standardizing the PCR for viral RNA in the plasma (viral load), and there are now commercial kits available. PCR is also important for determining whether the newborn of an HIV-positive mother is infected or not, as a complement to virus isolation.

In cases where an answer is needed immediately—for instance, when an organ transplant has to be performed—rapid diagnostic tests, some of which take but a few minutes, are useful complements to the conventional tests.

ELISA tests have been adapted to testing for antibodies in urine. The results have been entirely satisfactory, but the urine specimen must be preserved at $+4\,^{\circ}C$. Testing for antibodies in saliva is easy: the saliva is placed on a blotter kept at room temperature and can be used for up to three weeks thereafter. These two approaches, which depart from conventional serology, are interesting in that they render the taking of blood samples unnecessary: significant savings could thus be made if used more widely, enabling developing countries to carry out tests at less cost. However, despite their ease of application they should not be made into tests for personal use without medical supervision, unlike the take-home pregnancy tests available in all pharmacies.

THE PROBLEM OF VIRUS VARIABILITY

Are there variants (subgroups) of the virus that elude the tests? The discovery of HIV-2 gave weight to this problem. There were some patients, West Africans from Guinea-Bissau, Ivory Coast, and the Cape Verde Islands, who showed all the clinical signs of AIDS but whose Western blot serological profiles were incomplete; no conclusions could be drawn based on the international guidelines. Isolating the virus from the blood of some of these patients led to the discovery of antibodies to all the proteins of this new viral group, called HIV-2. The proteins of HIV-2 are slightly different in size from those of HIV-1, and most of the ELISA tests now available make it possible to recognize the two different viruses.

In similar circumstances, several laboratories recently isolated a new virus variant in AIDS patients who either were themselves from Central Africa (particularly Cameroon) or had sex partners from these countries. The envelope proteins were very different from those of HIV-1, and still more different from HIV-2 proteins.

Together with some colleagues from the hospitals of Reims and the Pitié-Salpêtrière, we recently isolated a virus of this type from the blood of a French female patient. This virus and other isolates of the same type do not constitute an HIV-3, but rather a subgroup of HIV-1 called HIV-O. Certain tests, particularly those that use synthetic peptides, had trouble detecting this new subgroup.

The existence of many subgroups in Africa suggests that each of the various different isolates of HIV has a distinct, ancient origin. It confirms that HIV viruses have long been present in humans, since well before the epidemic was detected. The list of these subgroups is probably not complete. Before declaring the absence of HIV in a patient showing the symptoms of AIDS, it is therefore necessary to perform all the detection tests currently in existence.

We have studied a number of patients showing all the symptoms of AIDS but in whom we could find no trace of HIV. In one patient we isolated a mycoplasma, *Mycoplasma fermentans,* without, however, being able to determine formally the causal role of this infectious agent. One must not forget that humans, like many mammals, carry retroviral sequences embedded in their hereditary material, which are apparently easily tolerated by the body. We cannot rule out the possibility that, in certain pathological conditions, the presence of the proteins derived from these endogenous sequences, if in excessive amounts, might weaken the immune system. If so, this sort of "AIDS" would not be transmissible. Epidemiological studies conducted by WHO on a certain number of cases have not been able to prove any transmission in these instances of "AIDS without HIV."

The Evolution of the Disease

Every patient has his or her own history. However, studies conducted on well-characterized, closely followed patient groups have helped delineate certain constants in the evolution of the disease (that is, its progression within the patient).

It is usually a long evolution: after infection with HIV, about ten years on average pass before clinical and biological signs become manifest. The natural history of the disease includes three well-defined stages: primary infection, the silent phase, and clinical illness. In a certain number of cases, primary infection manifests itself by an acute condition with commonplace, flu-like symptoms lasting from a few days to several weeks. In other cases no overt symptoms develop, and the primary infection passes unnoticed. We now know that the body's reaction to this primary infection determines the course of the infection (to be discussed shortly). Then comes a silent, intermediate phase, which may last years without clinical symptoms. During this phase, minor biological anomalies begin to appear over time, becoming gradually more severe. Until a few years ago, this period was considered a period of latency: the virus was assumed to be "sleeping" in the cells it had infected. We now know that it continues to be active and to multiply in certain cells. Finally, the immune system becomes severely disturbed and can no longer perform its functions; opportunistic diseases begin to appear, as well as certain forms of cancer. This, then, is full-blown AIDS.

The differences between individual cases, however, are important. The longest followup of a group includes 6,704 homosexuals and bisexuals from San Francisco, recruited between 1978 and 1980 for a hepatitis B vaccination trial. Nine percent of them were infected with HIV: 1 percent of these had developed AIDS within two years, 12 percent within five years, 51 percent within ten years, and 68 percent within thirteen years and eight months (latest statistics as of 1998). 113 of the seropositives (HIV-positive patients) had not developed AIDS after thirteen years. The evolution is quite similar in smaller populations: both among hemophiliacs, for whom we usually know the precise dates of infection, and among intravenous drug users, about whom we have less information. We may therefore conclude that the incubation period of the disease is roughly the same regardless of the manner in which the person is infected. The person's age, however, may influence the life span: the older one is at the moment of infection, the more rapid the progress of the disease. It has also been observed that the closer a seropositive blood donor is to having full-blown AIDS, the more swiftly a transfusion recipient of this donor's blood will develop the disease. The same is true for HIV-positive mothers who infect their infants: the more advanced their stage of the disease, the more their children are at risk of being infected. In both cases, a significant quantity of virus is transmitted at the moment of infection. As for intravenous drug users, it is more difficult to obtain reliable data, because the drugs themselves undermine the immune system, and these patients' opportunistic infections may be different from those of the homosexuals who currently serve as our reference base. Drug users often suffer from septicemia (blood poisoning), which can cause death. We cannot say today how many infected people will still be alive twenty years after infection. Perhaps 5 or 10 percent. We lack the necessary perspective to answer such a question.

How can we explain these sorts of differences? Several factors play a role: they include the very nature of the virus; its potential for variability; the quantity of virus received at the time of infection; and the response of the body, especially the reaction of the immune system at the moment of infection. Other infectious agents may also play a role by activating the immune system, which would increase the number of target cells (cells for the virus to infect) and/or activate cells holding the virus in a latent state.

Whatever the case, this long evolution for a viral infection is not peculiar to human AIDS. We find it as well in monkeys infected by SIV and in animals infected by other slow viruses such as Visna virus in sheep, infectious anemia virus in horses, and encephalitis virus in goats. Another human retrovirus, HTLV, is the source of a form of leukemia that appears dozens of years after infection. A degenerative brain disease called tropical spastic paraparesis also seems linked to infection by this retrovirus and occurs after a long incubation period.

The Early Phase: Primary Infection

The first weeks following infection by the virus now seem to play a determining role in the evolution of the disease, whatever the manner of infection: sexual, blood-related, or perinatal (around the time of birth). At first an acute, or primary, infection occurs, lasting usually a few weeks. The virus first meets some cells present in the mucous membranes called dendritic cells. Such cells are capable of migration and when loaded with virus, will pass it to monocytes, which circulate throughout the blood and the lymph system. Finally the virus will reproduce in a sustained manner in the lymph glands, the first barriers against infectious agents, but will reproduce little in the blood. This is why it is difficult to isolate the virus at this stage.

This phase may be clinically silent, but it is often characterized by nonspecific signs of acute viral infection that resemble flu symptoms, which is why such an episode often goes unnoticed. A combination of symptoms may, however, occur over a period ranging from one to more than four weeks: fever and skin lesions are the most common, but there are also headaches, muscle and joint pains, diarrhea, sore throat. More infrequently, alarming signs may occur, such as swollen lymph nodes, or neurological changes indicating the virus has entered the brain, but these symptoms go away by themselves. At this stage, the patient rarely seeks medical help for what are apparently harmless symptoms, though a later investigation by the doctor can help to date the time of infection.

Recent studies suggest that the time it takes to develop full-blown AIDS is linked to the severity of symptoms during the primary infection.

The immune response during primary infection occurs in several steps that are in no way specific to AIDS. First the macrophages intervene, followed by a secretion of interferon, then a cellular immune response, and finally a humoral immune response, the appearance of antibodies. We shall now consider these events in more detail.

Monocytes (cells present in the bloodstream) are the first to respond, coming quickly to the site of infection to meet the intruder head-on. They then transform into macrophages: large, cells capable of phagocytosis (engulfing cells). Through absorption and then digestion, the macrophages attempt to destroy the infected cells. The problem with HIV is that it can easily replicate itself in macrophages, so the more the macrophages multiply in order to digest the virus, the more the virus multiplies.

Very soon, then, we observe a *secretion of interferon*. This involves a group of special proteins that serve to defend the body against all forms of virus. Any cell infected by a virus will secrete interferon, which is supposed to neutralize the virus. This is also true of macrophages and lymphocytes, the two main targets for infection by HIV.

One to two weeks later, the *cellular immune response* occurs: "killer" cells (usually T8 lymphocytes) appear. Their mission is to destroy the infected cells. Though they actually have no effect on the virus itself, they recognize, on the surface of the infected cells, the envelope proteins and internal proteins of the virus.

It would appear that the secretion of interferon and the cellular immune response are the most efficient means of reducing the production of the virus at the moment of primary infection.

The last immune response is the *secretion of antibodies* by the B lymphocytes. Currently, this response is useful in laboratory detection, since we do not yet have any practical way of easily detecting other immune responses or replication of the virus itself. Given these circumstances, one can understand why infection can only be detected a few weeks after infection, since that is when the antibodies first appear.

The virus multiplies in the macrophages and the activated lymphocytes. Normally, the lymphocytes are at rest. They are only activated when a foreign particle enters. If, at the time of exposure to HIV, the person has another infection as well, the already activated lymphocytes facilitate infection by HIV. This has been observed, for example, in cases of infection through sex in women already afflicted with a genital infection, where their mucous membranes showed a significant quantity of activated lymphocytes and macrophages.

At the early stage of infection, the virus does not kill the cells it infects. As mentioned earlier, it must respect the integrity of the cell, so that the cell may produce as many viral particles as possible, which will then infect new cells in turn. Most often, the person is infected by a pool of viral particles, some of which are more virulent than others. The most virulent disappear during the first days of infection: the cells they infect are destroyed preemptively by the cytotoxic T8 lymphocytes or else die prematurely from the viral infection itself. It is as though, at the beginning of the infection, *a selection were taking place that favors the weak viral strains over the strong ones.*[3] In fact, this arrangement benefits only those best able to multiply without killing the host cells and which can best hide from the immune system. It is only when the immune system is destroyed that the more virulent strains reappear, the ones that kill the cells directly.

During this period, biological testing shows a decrease in the number of T4 lymphocytes due to multiplication of the virus. This is the most significant biological phenomenon of HIV infection. The quantity of T4 lymphocytes is easy to determine: this is regularly done by taking blood from HIV-positive patients who live according to the rhythms of their fluctuations. Initially, the total number is the same as in a healthy HIV-negative person: about a thousand trillion (10^{15}) lymphocytes circulating throughout the body, or 500 to 1,200 per cubic millimeter of blood. This number gradually decreases by about 60 to 100 per cubic millimeter annually in these patients. Normally, humans have twice as many T4 as T8 lymphocytes in the blood; from the start of the infection, this ratio gradually reverses until, at the stage of full-blown AIDS, the T4 lymphocytes have all but disappeared. An objective, though variable, indicator of the presence of HIV is the viral antigen p24 in the blood. As for the antibodies, when they exist, they appear over the course of the three-month period following exposure to the virus.

The Intermediate Phase: Asymptomatic Period

Following the primary infection is a period of several years called the asymptomatic, intermediate, or chronic phase. The infected person usually shows no clinical signs, but can pass the virus on to others and should be under regular medical supervision. Antibodies can be found in the blood, but little or no virus. In most cases, walnut-sized lymph nodes persist, as was the case for BRU.

A lymph node has a double role. It is a barrier against infection, but it also acts as a reservoir for the virus, as do all the other organs in the body that produce lymphocytes such as the spleen, the tonsils, and Peyer's patches in the intestines. In these tissues, dendritic cells filter out the virus, which then accumulates. At this stage, the virus reproduces slowly and most likely passes from cell to cell unbeknownst to the immune system. Little by little, the T4 lymphocytes become infected in turn, and the deterioration of the immune system begins.

The asymptomatic phase is especially important to researchers: the better we can understand what happens during these years, the more we will be able to forestall the onset of illness. For once AIDS develops, therapeutic intervention is more difficult.

For a long time, researchers and clinicians wondered whether the infection actually evolved during this period, or remained "asleep" in the lymphocytes. In the early 1980s, we questioned whether all HIV-positive people would develop AIDS. We now know that almost all will. In fact, some cells are continuously infected by the virus, especially in the lymph nodes.

What factors influence the duration of the silent phase? The virus itself certainly plays an important role: certain strains have strong reproductive capabilities, others do not. The quantity of virus present during the phase of acute primary infection must also be taken into consideration. On the other hand, the immune system's response during the primary infection also matters: if a significant amount of virus is produced in the blood and the lymphatic tissues, the evolution toward AIDS is swift. If on the other hand the immune response has been very effective, the virus disappears entirely from the blood and almost entirely from the lymph glands, and the asymptomatic phase is very long.

In the case of slow evolution, the problem becomes even more complex. What is it that makes the HIV-positive condition evolve toward AIDS? When the immune response is good, only a very small amount of virus remains. Why, then, is the immune system imperiled? Why does the disease evolve differently in patients endowed with comparable immune systems, and why do they respond to treatments differently? And why do we sometimes find so little virus in certain patients, even ones with full-blown AIDS? All these questions suggest that different cofactors may come into play during evolution of the disease, a point we shall return to. For now it is enough to note that, although the role of HIV in AIDS is acknowledged by everyone (or almost everyone), a great many unknowns still remain in the story of this illness, which has no equal among human diseases. AIDS is most often heralded by the appearance of minor clinical signs and by certain biological changes. It is usually through the emergence of outbreaks on the skin or mucous membranes (oral candidiasis, shingles, leukoplakia of the tongue, acne, impetigo) that HIV-positive patients discover their condition. These infections are minor but troublesome, since they recur in spite of treatments. No doubt this is due already to a deficiency in the immune system's response to omnipresent agents. In the body, the effect of antibiotics is normally complemented by the work of the immune system; here the system has been weakened. Allergic reactions, in the form of rashes and itching, may also occur.

At this stage, biological tests show several changes. The number of T8 lymphocytes and immunoglobulins (antibody molecules) increases. There is a general activation of the immune system resulting in the death of cells from apoptosis (a process of cellular "suicide" described in detail in Chapter 7). There is also the release of beta-2 microglobulin (a component of the histocompatibility antigens, of HLA, on the surface of cells); the proportion of beta-2 microglobulin increases in the blood as the T4 lymphocytes decrease. Interferon begins to circulate, but unlike its role at the start of infection, its effect is henceforth harmful. Indeed, the body does not know how to react to a chronic viral infection. Interferon can be compared to a braking system. If you were to drive continuously with your foot on the brake pedal, the whole system would heat up. Interferon is an effective brake for an isolated occurrence, but it is not adaptable to a chronic condition. Not only does it lose its effectiveness; it may contribute to the erosion of the immune system, as does the secretion of other inflammatory cytokines, the regulatory molecules used by cells.

Concurrent infections—such as cytomegalovirus, hepatitis B, and mycoplasmas—seem to play an important role at this stage. Depression of the immune system is not yet general, but begins with commensal germs, those habitually present in the body. Normally, the immune system handles them perfectly well: they multiply just enough to remind the immune system, which then thwarts them. Upon infection with HIV, the lymphocytes activated by these germs can be selectively infected and destroyed by the virus, diminishing the body's immunity to these agents, which will later become the source of opportunistic infections (pneumocystosis, toxoplasmosis, cytomegalovirus, candidiasis, and mycoplasmas, among others).

The biological warning signals then light up, differently in different patients, indicating that the clinical phase is approaching. The amount of virus in the lymphocytes and blood increases. More virulent variants of the virus begin to appear, causing the infected cells to fuse with each other: the deadly virus can no longer be contained by the immune system.

The Final Phase: Full-blown AIDS

AIDS arrives with the appearance of one or several opportunistic infections: the most frequently occurring in Western countries are pneumocystosis and toxoplasmosis. In Africa, tuberculosis and cryptococcosis (a fungal disease that often manifests as meningitis) are the most frequent. Cancers such as lymphomas and Kaposi's sarcoma can also appear. In 40 percent of the cases, the nervous system is attacked by the virus itself or by an opportunistic infectious agent. These illnesses signal the failure of the immune system.

By definition, an opportunistic infection cannot develop in a person with normal immune defenses. In AIDS, several such infections can develop simultaneously. They can even affect the same organ—the brain, for example. Since cellular immunity is particularly affected, it is often intracellular germs that cause these infections.

Such infections are characterized by their seriousness and their potential for recurrence. Fortunately, many antibiotics are effective in preventing as well as curing them. This has prompted the establishment of prophylactic (preventive) measures for some of them (toxoplasmosis, pneumocystosis, tuberculosis and other mycobacterial infections) even before the first infectious episode has occurred, and then afterward, to prevent recurrence.

The nature of opportunistic infections depends on the prevalence of their causative agents within the surrounding general population. In Africa, tuberculosis is predominant. In the United States, Canada, and Europe, it is pneumocystosis. In France, toxoplasmosis is equally as prevalent as pneumocystosis, being apparently linked to the consumption of undercooked meat.[4] In Southeast Asia, a fungus *(Penicillium marneffei)* causes serious skin infections. The relative frequency of these infections over the last few years has been altered, however, thanks to various prophylactic treatments as well as to the triple anti-retroviral therapy (a potent combination of two traditional reverse transcriptase inhibitors with the newly developed protease inhibitors). The result has been to extend the lives of the sick.

The immune system holds numerous pretumor cells in check. When it weakens, some cells develop to form Kaposi's sarcoma, or lymphomas specifically related to the Epstein-Barr virus.[5]

The nervous system is also very often affected. At the moment of primary infection, this may take the form of encephalitis (described below), meningitis (brain membrane infection), or an attack on the peripheral nerves. All these episodes go away by themselves. It is known that certain strains of the virus have a greater affinity for macrophages than for lymphocytes. Once infected, the macrophages cross the meningeal membrane protecting the brain and create small centers of viral infection.

At the onset of full-blown AIDS, these centers are reactivated by the collapse of the immune system. In the absence of treatment, encephalitis thus develops in about 20 percent of all patients. The first signs are difficulties in concentration, gaps in memory, and a general intellectual slowdown. Gradually, over the course of a few months or even a few weeks, a state of dementia takes over. In different tests, the brain is found to have lost some of its white matter and sometimes becomes atrophied. This encephalitis is the most common neurological complication at the AIDS stage. Forty to 80 percent of all AIDS patients have neurological symptoms of varying degrees of severity. A very serious form of this infection occurs in newborns of HIV-positive mothers; these babies show significant immune deficiencies, and the prognosis is very bleak in all cases.

The question arises as to how the virus creates these disorders without infecting the neurons. It is believed that it does this through indirect mechanisms. The macrophages secrete inflammatory cytokines that greatly disturb the functioning of the glial cells (making up the myelin sheath that wraps around the neurons), or release oxidation products, particularly nitric oxide. In small amounts, nitric oxide is a messenger between nerve cells; in large amounts, it is a poison that prevents their functioning. Researchers recently showed that the virus could infect glial cells in culture. These cells feed neurons; any harm to them could directly alter the neurons' functioning or bring about their death by apoptosis. In addition, glial cells infected by HIV produce the Nef protein, as discussed earlier.

The nervous system is also the site of opportunistic infections: cerebral toxoplasmosis (in 14 percent of the cases), cytomegaloviral meningitis, neuromeningeal cryptococcosis (19 percent of the cases), lymphomas, and even multifocal leukoencephalitis, caused by a small DNA virus (whose genome consists of DNA).

A variety of disturbances in the blood can likewise occur as AIDS follows its course: a decrease in the number of blood platelets, with resultant problems in clotting; the alteration in the stem cells of bone marrow; and the presence of autoantibodies (antibodies directed against the body's own tissues) in the blood.

At this stage of the disease, all elements of the immune system collapse. The lymphocytes are killed by the virus or die of apoptosis. A sharp decline in T4 lymphocytes sometimes precedes the onset of an opportunistic infection. Which of these two factors determines the other? The opportunistic infection, by stimulating the lymphocytes, increases the risk of infection by the virus.

In addition, in every cell, a destructive process called oxidative stress begins to accelerate: The activated and infected macrophages release greater and greater quantities of oxidation products, free radicals, into the bloodstream. These are toxic to the other cells; they induce apoptosis and breakups of DNA and modify the membranes of other cells, which then become much more fragile. This mechanism causes significant cellular destruction. In the terminal phase, there are no longer any T4 lymphocytes in the blood while large quantities of viral antigen are circulating. The patient can die from the recurrence of an infection, a cancer, an encephalopathy (brain disease), or from cachexia (wasting syndrome).

This final stage is quite typical of AIDS. There is a tremendous deterioration of the muscles, and weight loss accelerates. Another source of this phenomenon is malnutrition. Directly or indirectly, the virus greatly affects the digestive tract: the products of digestion are not as well absorbed by the intestine. The epithelial cells, which line the intestines and whose role is to absorb the nutrients necessary to the body's functioning, are not, however, directly infected by the virus. But they suffer from the fact that the Peyer's patches, situated just beneath the epithelium, contain infected lymphocytes, which secrete cytokines that greatly disturb their functioning. Gradually the products of digestion are no longer absorbed. The infection also probably has a direct or indirect effect on the muscle fibers, attacking the mitochondria, organelles within each cell that are necessary to its functioning, since they provide it with chemical energy. The muscles atrophy affecting those of the face first.

There is much to be learned from observing long-term survivors, or rather, slow progressors. These are people who were infected more than ten or fifteen years ago in some cases, and who still show no sign of the disease. Their biological parameters are stable, even though their number of T4 lymphocytes falls by about 65 per cubic millimeter annually. In the San Francisco study cohort, a third of those testing HIV-positive have not progressed toward AIDS more than ten years after being infected. Many laboratories are interested in these patients and hope to determine what factors in them prevent or retard the pathogenic action of the virus. It seems that the cellular immune response (the T8 lymphocytes that kill cells infected by the virus) plays an important role, along with other still unidentified factors.

Is the Process Inescapable?

Are there cases where man's interaction with HIV is any different from what has been described so far? Can a person be rid of the virus entirely or develop a natural immunity to it? That seems possible, but such situations are certainly rare and difficult to study. There seem to be a few cases of so-called abortive infection. We can assume that in such a case the immune system was victorious in its struggle against the virus. The existence of such a situation, however rare, would lead us to think that it could be made more common with the right therapies. In other words, very early treatment, relating to proper stimulation of the immune system, might eradicate the infection.

Another particularly encouraging situation: that of regular sexual partners of seropositive subjects who remain seronegative, even though they do not take safe-sex precautions. In some of these people, studied by immunologists Gene Shearer and Mario Clerici, we can observe a cellular immune response to certain fragments of the viral envelope and specific antibodies in the mucous membranes without the appearance of regular antibodies in the blood. The fact that these people remain seronegative for so long leads us to think that this cellular immunity might have a protective effect. These results lend hope that one day we will be able to harness this natural immunity and universalize it through vaccination.

4

The History of an Epidemic

Mirko Grmek, in his 1990 book, *Histoire du SIDA*; puts the history of AIDS into some perspective: "In 1977, while AIDS was already incubating on American shores, William Beveridge, an excellent historian of diseases, published a work entitled *Influenza, the Last Great Plague*. He was wrong, of course, and yet he was partially correct: the flu is in fact the last of the classic types of plague. AIDS, an unforeseen epidemic that, indeed, could not have been foreseen within the framework of traditional nosology [the classification of diseases], is the first postmodern plague.

But is AIDS a new disease? Put so bluntly, this question elicits equivocal and contradictory answers. Yes, AIDS is a new disease inasmuch as it was not even conceivable before the 1970s. A disease used to be defined either by its symptoms or by the damage it caused to anatomical structures. Neither definition applied to AIDS, a disease without specific clinical symptoms, characterized by invisible subcellular damage and caused by a germ that could not be detected even by the most up-to-date means of analysis. Yes, AIDS is a new disease in its current pandemic dimension. But at the same time, it is not really a new disease inasmuch as its causal agent has existed for a very long time and behind the screen of other infectious diseases has been the source of sporadic and even collective pathological conditions, though these remained very limited in space and time.[1]

↝ BIOLOGICAL studies conducted retrospectively on blood samplings taken in the 1960s and thereafter, as well as certain clinical descriptions, indicate that the AIDS virus was present in humans well before we started talking about this disease. It is difficult to go farther back in time, but it is also certain that viruses closely related to HIV existed earlier in nonhuman primates. How do we explain that it suddenly started ravaging entire areas of the globe, reaching epidemic proportions? What triggered this process? If AIDS is indeed, as Grmek calls it, "the first postmodern plague," it is essential to understand the respective origins of the virus and the epidemic. Today the virus has been isolated, and detection tests are now reliable. Tracing the origin of the epidemic is therefore less important now than it was when, in tracking its spread, we were looking for the virus itself. The point is not to incriminate a particular group (ethnic or otherwise), country, or "person responsible." What matters most is to understand the exact origins of the virus and the conditions that made its explosion possible, so we may avoid the occurrence of new epidemics of this sort. For this reason it is important to distinguish between the origin of the virus and that of the epidemic.

THE ORIGIN OF THE VIRUS

Viruses are very ancient parasites, probably as ancient as the cells that harbor them. Even bacteria have their own viruses, called bacteriophages. There are two theories, which in fact are not mutually exclusive, as to the possible origin of viruses. One says that they may have come from the breakdown of more complicated organisms, small bacteria that lived in a symbiotic relationship with cells. With time, these bacteria may have lost certain functions, such as the structural and enzymatic equipment necessary for manufacturing proteins from messenger RNAs. This theory is probably valid for the larger viruses, particularly smallpox (variola) and cowpox (attenuated bovine variola).

According to the second hypothesis, viruses resulted from the gradually increasing autonomy of certain cellular genes, particularly those that code for the replication enzymes of nucleic acids. This probably explains the origin of retroviruses. We know, moreover, that the genomes of the higher species, including man, contain perfectly integrated sequences closely related to retroviruses which can change position on the genome and carry away flanking genes with them. These integrated sequences are called retrotransposons.

HIV belongs to a particular subgroup of retroviruses that are never passed on vertically (that is, from generation to generation), but only through horizontal transmission, from one subject to another. Similar viruses, called simian immunodeficiency viruses (SIV), have been isolated in some African monkeys. But the monkeys infected naturally by these viruses tolerate them very well and are not immunosuppressed, probably because the parasite, in its long period of adaptation to its hosts, has selected resistant individuals and viruses of moderate replication. Infected species include the mangabey monkey, green monkeys, and mandrills. The strain of SIV infecting the mangabeys of West Africa is very close in sequence to HIV-2 but does not produce illness in mangabeys; however, it does seem to be the virus that induces AIDS in farm-bred macaques. Macaques, monkeys living in Asia, are not infected in the wild.

The geographic localization of the mangabey corresponds roughly to the West African focus (the region of most outbreaks) of HIV-2. But very few monkeys living in the wild are infected by SIV. Often these little monkeys were captured by villagers upon the death of their mothers and then partially tamed. People might have become infected during play with the animals, through bites, for example. It is thus possible that HIV-2 was transmitted accidentally to humans by these monkeys. But this hypothesis has not been definitively proved.

Not only could the mangabey virus have infected man, but it seems to have been passed on, also accidentally, to macaque monkeys at the start of the 1970s in American primate breeding centers. In the macaque, SIV attacks the same lymphocytes as HIV does in humans, and the biochemical and biological properties of its proteins very closely resemble those of HIV. It induces an illness that manifests itself in opportunistic infections and lymphomas, and is therefore very similar to human AIDS.

Why does SIV cause illness in the macaque but not in the mangabey? There is no clear answer to this question. It is possible the mangabey has been infected for many generations and has adapted to it. A mutation of the CD4 receptor may have occurred in certain individuals that enabled them to survive viral infection. This would explain why the mangabeys seem to be in some way protected. On the other hand, when the virus is passed on accidentally to other primates (man and macaques) who have not been previously infected by it, it unleashes a disease.

HIV-2 is associated with AIDS cases, but it is less pathogenic than HIV-1 and more difficult to pass on from mother to child and through sexual contacts. Moreover, its incubation period is probably longer. We know today that HIV-2 also occurs outside of West Africa; about a hundred cases of infection have been recorded in Europe and the United States as well. Still another focus was recently found in the Bombay region of India; prostitutes were the first to be affected. The virus was probably spread through human relations between natives of Mozambique and western India. Former Portuguese colonies have in fact maintained commercial exchange networks among themselves, and all of them, like Mozambique, have been infected by HIV-2, though the epidemic exploded after decolonization. Indeed, one can follow the extent of the virus from the Cape Verde Islands, Guinea-Bissau, and Príncipe Island and São Tomé off the coast of equatorial West Africa, all the way to Angola, whose population is as infected by HIV-1 as by HIV-2. We find HIV-2 again in Mozambique, on the other side of Africa, and from there it moves on to India. Although HIV-2 is less virulent (slower to develop into symptoms) than HIV-1, it is very important to follow closely its epidemic progression. Once fully developed, the AIDS caused by HIV-2 is just as grave as that caused by HIV-1.

The origin of HIV-1 is even more mysterious. One is tempted to look for an animal source as with HIV-2, some primate infected with the virus but not sick. For a long time this approach produced no results whatsoever: none of the viruses isolated in monkeys tested in Africa was close to HIV-1. The situation changed in the early 1990s, when one virus and then a second were isolated in chimpanzees. This type of isolate was named SIV-CPZ (CPZ for chimpanzee).

In Gabon, the Elf Aquitaine oil company and the government made an agreement whereby part of the royalties received for petroleum concessions would be used for the creation and maintenance of a research center in Franceville for the study of the sexually transmitted diseases causing the high rate of sterility in Gabonese women. This center keeps a large number of primates lodged on its premises. It was here that research scientist Eric Delaporte first isolated SIV-CPZ, which was later cloned and sequenced by Simon Wain-Hobson's team at the Pasteur Institute. To date, this is the simian virus closest to HIV-1. Another viral isolate was made from a chimpanzee illegally imported into Holland from Zaire. From it, a team from the Institute of Tropical Medicine at Antwerp isolated another virus closely related to the first CPZ virus.[2]

It is reasonable to look for a geographic correlation between HIV-1 and the chimpanzee, similar to that existing between HIV-2 and the mangabey monkey. It has been noted that there are two areas of wild chimpanzees in what remains of the African tropical rainforest: one in Gabon, the other in Zaire. The virus that has been found in infected Zairians may have come from the chimpanzees of Zaire. How then do we explain the fact that Gabon remains only slightly infected by HIV-1, even though there are infected chimpanzees there? It is true, of course, that Gabon is much less populous than Zaire. For an epidemic to develop, it is necessary for the virus to multiply intensively and for a significant mix of the population to effect multiple transmission. These conditions were all present in Zaire but much less so in Gabon.

In fact, the animal origin of the virus is far from proven. Other hypotheses are also possible. The virus may have existed in humans for a very long time in different regions of the world, in a sporadic state, without creating epidemics. Certain strains may come from Africa, but others may have had different origins and been transmitted sporadically from one individual to another. We now have the sequences of a large number of isolates from different parts of the world. It is therefore possible to classify the various strains by homology, that is, by comparing certain parts of their sequences—that of the envelope, for example. Divergence becomes greater as the virus multiplies and spreads. If it is present in only a few individuals, it varies little; if it is passed on successively to a large number of people, it changes a great deal. Thus the great diversification of HIV-1 is not necessarily a sign that it is ancient; it may merely be a sign of intense replication.) Today, nine subtypes of the major group HIV-1 plus the new subgroup HIV-O have been identified, but the list is far from complete. It is therefore possible the virus existed in an endemic state (that is, at a low level) on several continents before developing into an epidemic.

If we grant that the virus has been present in humans for a long time, in Africa and probably elsewhere, the question then arises as to why the epidemic is so recent. Why, in just a few years, has the same virus gone from being a sporadic infection to an explosive epidemic?

THE ORIGIN OF THE EPIDEMIC

Often, as with plague or cholera, epidemics have spread as a result of transportation. A germ enters a new population and wreaks havoc because the immune systems of the affected people are not at all adapted to fighting it.

An epidemic develops when the incubation period is long enough to allow a significant transmission of the germ to other individuals, especially if it is transmitted sexually. Generally speaking, it is not in any germ's "interest" to kill its host too easily or quickly since that would stop the epidemic. In the case of AIDS, which is essentially transmitted through sexual relations, the fact that the incubation period is so long makes numerous transmissions possible. The variants of the virus that might cause a sudden manifestation of AIDS are eliminated, since the persons infected by such variants would die before being able to pass them on through sexual contacts.

On the other hand, the epidemic spreads all the more easily as numerous people come into contact with the germ. For AIDS, the groups of homosexuals with multiple partners no doubt had an impact on the growth of the epidemic in the United States, as did other key groups in Africa.

The disease seems to predate the current epidemic. The oldest described case, an American, dates from 1952. According to tests performed retrospectively or through tracking of viral DNA in frozen serum, a sailor from Manchester, England, in 1959 and a young adolescent from Missouri in 1968 have also been identified. The first observations of AIDS in patients from Africa were made in 1981 and 1982 in Paris and Brussels. Grmek mentions some cases of aggressive Kaposi's sarcoma in equatorial Africa starting around 1950 and more importantly, the presence, around the start of the 1960s, of a highly malignant form of Kaposi's sarcoma accompanied by meningitis and deadly pneumonia in seasonal laborers traveling from the central regions to South Africa. The African epidemic, however, did not really break out until the autumn of 1982. It was around this time that interest in this part of the world began to grow. In Uganda, in the village of Rakai (with 500 inhabitants), notice was taken of a group of seventeen smugglers who died from intestinal disturbances. Explanations were immediately offered: the disease came from outsiders, from Tanzanians, and was divine punishment for the sins of those it struck down.

Very quickly, as we can see, blame was laid on exchanges between countries and even between continents. In the United States, a patient "zero" was even identified. A flight steward for Air Canada, "a great traveller and handsome lad rather free with his charms, [he sowed] disease and death at every one of his destinations, at the rate of about two hundred fifty partners yearly," writes Grmek.[3] It is doubtful, however, that the American epidemic could have developed from a single patient.

For Westerners, it was tempting to attribute the origin of

HIV to Africa, whence it was supposedly carried abroad via intercontinental air transportation. Similarly, there was much talk of Haitians at the start of the epidemic. Several thousand Haitians had in fact been to Zaire for extended stays in the early 1960s and later returned to their native country. Thus was born the hypothesis that they had brought HIV to their island and then passed it on to North American tourists. This is rather unlikely, since the virus seems to have come to Haiti much more recently than to the mainland. In Quebec, for example, there have been two waves of Haitian immigration. The Haitians of the first wave, in the 1960s, were not infected with the virus, unlike the immigrants of the second wave in the 1980s.

It is more likely the infection was spread in the opposite manner. Haiti, like the other Caribbean islands, may well have been infected by tourists from North America. In this scenario, the virus may have traveled directly from Africa to North America: in the 1970s, in fact, advertisements in American gay magazines offered tours in Zaire, specifically in Kinshasa.

Many epidemiologists believe the virus was "taken out" of its African niche by social and cultural factors. The epidemic's origins, by this reasoning, lie in the transformation of our societies: the AIDS virus did not change; rather, the population became more sensitive to it. Medicine, keeping most infectious diseases in check through vaccinations and antibiotics, left the field open to other epidemics. And such practices as injections and transfusions, due to the use of unsterilized needles, actually favored their development.

Most importantly, social phenomena related to the mixing of populations facilitated the rapid spread of the virus through sexual contact. In Western countries, there was the sexual liberation that accompanied the widespread use of oral contraceptives, and the acceptance of homosexuality; in the third world, there was the breakup of traditional communities,

brought on by economic and social development. All these social and cultural factors facilitated the sequential transmission
and selection of the pathogenic virus.

This sort of explanation, however, is incomplete. It is legitimate to ask what made a virus that already existed so virulent.

There is a biological theory about this. It is unlikely that a
single mutation increasing the germ's virulence could have
taken place, since all the variants of HIV, including HIV-2,
would have to have mutated at the same time. More likely, a biological cofactor, such as a new species of mycoplasma, may
have emerged to act synergistically with the virus. The mycoplasma could have appeared in certain communities of
multiple-partner homosexuals and resisted prolonged antibiotic treatments. There are some solid epidemiological arguments today indicating that a new, previously unrecognized
species *(Mycoplasma penetrans)* is present in a high incidence of
HIV-positive patients in the United States, Europe, and Africa.
Gay American tourists could have brought this mycoplasma to
Zaire and in turn brought HIV back from Africa to America.
If this cofactor is essential to the virulence of HIV, then we
should find it in all the parts of the world where HIV infection
is present, since it would be transmitted with the virus. Only
an in-depth epidemiological study would make it possible to
evaluate its role. Still, other varieties of mycoplasma could have
had the same effect. The investigation must therefore extend to
the other species as well, or even search for another agent.

INFECTION

Why did the disease break out primarily among homosexuals?
If the epidemic has become as vast as it has, this is because homosexual relations more effectively transmit the germ and

above all because certain gays had many partners at the start of the 1980s. Indeed, it is anal-genital relations that constitute the most significant risk, while any activity likely to traumatize the mucous membranes of the anus increases the risk of contagion. And this increases in turn with the number of partners one has. Use of the recreational drug amyl nitrite (in the form commonly called "poppers") during sex was a further risk factor at the start of the epidemic, probably because it dilates the blood vessels. Present and past sexually transmitted diseases are also significant risk factors, especially genital ulcers, syphilis, and gonorrhea. Oral-genital relations carry less risk, although not negligibly so. There have in fact been cases of transmission through fellatio.

The use of intravenous drugs is the second means of HIV transmission in the United States and Europe, with infection occurring through the sharing or reuse of needles tainted with contaminated blood. According to CDC statistics, of the approximately 700,000 AIDS cases in the United States, about 160,000 were infected through intravenous drug use. In Europe, this mode of transmission is particularly prevalent in Italy and Spain, and in France as well, where it continues to increase. In Bari and Milan in Italy, between 1980 and 1985 the percentage of HIV-positives among drug addicts rose from 4 to 76 percent. In France, there are as many as 30,000 HIV-positives, and drug addicts represent 25 percent of the number of known AIDS cases.[4]

The incidence of AIDS infection among drug addicts is over 50 percent in almost all the major cities of the Western world. Intravenous drug use triggered the epidemic in certain Southeast Asian countries, Thailand in particular. In addition, such drugs as cocaine and heroin diminish immunity and promote careless sexual practices, thus facilitating infection in ways besides transfer of infected blood.

To reduce the risks, drug substitution programs are essential. The best-known substitute for heroin addiction is methadone, a synthetic opium derivative whose effect lasts for two days; it is ingested in the form of a syrup to avoid the use of syringes. Its detractors claim that methadone therapy merely replaces one dependency with another. Indeed, one must take methadone for what it is: not a radical treatment for drug addiction but a support and a way of limiting the use of syringes. Statistics bear out its usefulness: 70 percent of intravenous drug users taking methadone treatment stop using heroin within six months, and 92 percent stop after four or five years. In other respects, this sort of program promotes social reintegration and curbs delinquency.

The same is true for needle exchange programs, which are not an incitement to drug use as some detractors have claimed. The connection between the difficult access to syringes and the rise of hepatitis B and AIDS was made sadly clear in the 1980s in Great Britain. In Glasgow, where syringes were made easily accessible, the rate of HIV infection went from 4.8 percent in 1987 to 1.1 percent in 1990, but in Edinburgh, where the association of pharmacists recommended that its members not sell syringes to drug addicts, the rate of infection increased. In France, since syringes were made freely available in 1987, 60 to 80 percent of intravenous drug users have stopped sharing their needles. The risks of infection remain significant, however, when the drug addict is marginalized, excluded, and forced to hide.

Heterosexual transmission has become the most significant mode of infection worldwide, since it represents 90 percent of the reported cases. It is predominant in tropical and equatorial regions, and is on the rise in Western countries, even though homosexual practices and intravenous drug use still constitute the mode of transmission in the majority of cases there. HIV can be present in the sperm and seminal fluid in men and in the vaginal secretions of women, to say nothing of menstrual blood. The risk of heterosexual transmission varies according to a certain number of parameters, including the incidence of infection in the country or region one is in, the likelihood of encountering an infected partner, and the number of sexual partners one has over a given length of time. Using mathematical models, the rate of transmission by sexual contact can be evaluated. For example, in 1993 the risk was 1 in 1,000 for men in the United States, compared with 56 in 1,000 for women in Thailand. These figures should be multiplied by 3 or 5 in cases of prior episodes of sexually transmissible diseases. Other factors also come into play: the presence of other sexually transmissible diseases in either partner and the severity of the partner's infection, sexual relations during menstruation, anal intercourse, uncircumcised male organs, as well as the virulence of the particular strain of the virus.

When one of the partners in a couple is HIV-positive, there arises the problem of sexual transmission of the virus. It is twice as easily passed on from man to woman as vice versa, unless the woman is at an advanced stage of the disease. In that case, the risks are equal.

A European study group, researching HIV transmission in nine countries over a four-year period, analyzed 563 stable couples in which one partner was seropositive. This study's goal was to determine the risk factors of HIV transmission. In the end, the rate of new HIV infection was 12 percent for the men and 20 percent for the women; in other words, the transmission was almost twice as frequent from man to woman as from woman to man, a finding consistent with the figures customarily obtained in other investigations (with a rate of 15 to 30 percent among female partners of infected men). These findings are all the more staggering when one considers that all these couples went every six months to a doctor who examined them, informed them of the risks they were taking, and urged them to practice safe sex. Indeed, among the twenty-four couples in which the partner always used a condom, none of the women were infected. Among the twenty-four couples who used condoms only sporadically, six women became infected. This study convincingly demonstrates the effectiveness of condoms, which some have questioned.

A few years ago, there were ten infected men for every HIV-positive woman in the world. Today, according to UNAIDS (the U.N. Programme on HIV/AIDS), is evening out, even reversing itself. In Africa the proportion of HIV-positive women in the population varies from 5 to 30 percent, depending on the region. The total number of infected women is estimated to be 4 million, leaving behind 1.1 to 1.6 million orphans. It is in these regions and in certain Asian countries that the epidemic is growing the fastest, where girls and young women under age 25 are the most affected. In Southeast Asia the epidemic has been growing since the 1980s. It has struck, in succession, drug addicts, prostitutes, their clients, and women in general. In France it is estimated that there are now 25,000 to 30,000 HIV-positive women, with 4,000 new cases each year. The women are usually infected through sexual relations, most often with intravenous drug users.

A number of factors increasing the risk of transmission from men to women have been pointed out: anal sex, which, because of the fragility of the rectal mucous lining, enables the virus to pass into the bloodstream or to infect target cells present beneath the mucous membrane; the clinical condition of the man, since relations become more infectious the more advanced the stage of his illness; and the woman's age (after forty-five, the vaginal lining becomes thinner and more fragile, facilitating passage of the virus).

The role of genital infections is difficult to calculate, since it varies from study to study. A number of Western and African studies stress the dangers of the open sores associated with such infections, and the importance of early treatment for sexually transmitted diseases. But in addition to the visible illnesses, there are also latent, undetected diseases (caused by chlamydiae, *Candida albicans,* or mycoplasmas) that can increase the number of target cells available to the virus; similarly, sexual relations during a woman's period also favor transmission of the virus.

Because of their practices, prostitutes combine several risk factors: multiple partners, genital infections, sometimes drug addiction. A study conducted in the center and outskirts of Paris in 1992 showed differences of seropositivity depending on sexual practices, condom use, and drug addiction.

Whether HIV-positive or not, a woman is always confronted with the question of childbearing. Obviously it is not advisable for seropositive women, but it is always easier to talk about before pregnancy. The physician should inform potential mothers of the risk of transmitting the infection and disease to the child. He must evaluate the mother's state of health and that of her partner (including the current stage of the disease, and any past or present drug addiction), as well as the couple's environment, as they may soon have to assume responsibility for the child. Particularly difficult are those cases in which the woman is HIV-negative and the man HIV-positive.

Although the virus is primarily present in the inflammatory cells (lymphocytes and monocytes), its presence in sperm cells cannot be ruled out. There is legitimate reason, therefore, to doubt the usefulness of various attempts to purify the sperm cells of HIV-positive men and use them in artificial insemination. Some practitioners recommend that a couple use condoms for all relations except those during the woman's ovulation period, and then hope that the infection is not transmitted. In all good conscience, no doctor could recommend any of these techniques, as they all involve some degree of risk.

In 40 percent of the cases, the woman learns she is HIV-positive at the time of her first prenatal exam. It is an emotional catastrophe. Very often the episode in which she contracted the germ has been nearly forgotten and is considered of little importance. She must then assume the double burden of being seropositive and choosing whether or not to remain pregnant.

In many countries, family pressure and religious considerations play an important role in the decision to carry the pregnancy to term. Tradition and culture also carry weight. Often HIV-positive African women living in France, for example, decide to go through with their pregnancy.

The average rate of HIV transmission from mother to fetus is about 20 percent, with a somewhat lower rate in Europe and a higher one in Africa. In the majority of cases, transmission takes place at the end of the pregnancy, in delivery or during breast feeding. (The virus is present in the mother's milk, and the additional risk of infection during breast feeding is estimated by WHO to be between 10 and 20 percent.)

The mechanism by which the infant is infected during pregnancy is still unknown, as is the precise role of the placenta in infection. In any case, transmission depends on the evolution of the disease in the mother. The risk ranges from 15 percent if the mother is asymptomatic to 55 percent in cases of severe immune depression. Advanced age on the mother's part is considered an additional risk factor. These data are very important, for if a woman really wants to have a child, she should be advised to have it at an early stage of her illness and while she is still young.

There is also much debate among health-care practitioners about the best manner of delivery for HIV-positive mothers. In the case of twins, the first child is infected more often than the second. This is especially true if the delivery is by natural childbirth rather than cesarean section. Are we to conclude that all HIV-positive pregnant women should have cesareans? Whatever the case, a few simple rules should be followed during natural delivery: the genital passages should be disinfected during labor every four to six hours with a virucidal (virus-killing) substance of the benzal konium chloride type; forceps should be used with caution, and bloody episiotomies avoided; electrodes should not be put on the baby's cranium; the umbilical cord should be disinfected before cutting; and after birth the child should be immediately washed to remove the mother's blood.

It does not appear that carrying a pregnancy to term has any deleterious effect on the health of the mother, unless she has a CD4 protein count of less than 200 per millimeter during the final trimester. As for the fetus, there are many differing opinions regarding the effect of maternal seropositivity on its development. This is because other factors come into play independently of those related to the virus itself and to the varieties of strains; these include continued drug addiction, alcohol consumption, degree of social integration, the nutritional state of the mother, and the existence of another infectious disease. Seropositivity in itself does not seem to cause any particular complications during pregnancy (such as miscarriage, or malformation or growth retardation in the fetus). This is quite surprising, given that some women take as many as five or six medications, even though these are not recommended during pregnancy.

At birth, diagnosis of HIV by the usual means—ELISA and Western blot—is not possible, because the newborn carries the mother's antibodies, which have passed through the placenta. These disappear only gradually. The first diagnosis can be made only by using specialized techniques—isolating the virus, and using the polymerase chain reaction—(PCR)—several weeks after birth. All infected babies have a positive viral culture at six months, though the virus isolation technique is not widely used. It is only at fifteen months that one can be certain whether the baby is infected, but often by that time many babies are already showing signs of the illness.

The prenatal method that consists of drawing fetal blood from the umbilical cord, used for diagnosing other viral infections, becomes problematic with AIDS. First of all, the virus is transmitted late in the pregnancy: obviously, if there were a positive diagnosis at eight months, interrupting the pregnancy would be out of the question. And diagnosis would be appropriate only if health-care practitioners could be certain to avoid infecting the child when taking the mother's blood sample and if effective treatment were available.

In this particular circumstance, PCR is also not reliable because, paradoxically, it is *too* precise. Indeed, PCR gene amplification is so sensitive that it may cause a false-positive result in the blood sample, which may contain some of the mother's infected cells, erroneously indicating infection in the child.

There are still many unknowns in the area of mother-fetus transmission of the virus. Recent studies in the United States and Europe have, however, shown that if AZT (azidothymidine) is administered to HIV-positive women during pregnancy, the incidence of such transmission can be significantly reduced. Cesarean delivery and suppression of breast feeding bring the risk of transmission close to zero. These encouraging results will no doubt change our approach to pregnancy in the coming years. However, given the significant role of women in passing the virus on to their partners and children, a precise and broad effort must be made in the way of education. In some countries, steps toward fertility control are already being taken; this must be followed up with sex education, so that women may take charge of their own bodies.

The Spread of the Epidemic

The AIDS epidemic has thus far gone through three different waves in space and time.

Initially, in the United States, Canada, western Europe, Australia, and in parts of Latin America, the disease began to spread in the late 1970s by means of homosexual relations and intravenous drug use. Heterosexual infection was still rare.

In the second wave, after 1980, the situation changed: the most significant advance now affected the heterosexual population. In sub-Saharan Africa, most victims have been infected through heterosexual relations. At the start of this wave of the epidemic, there were an equal number of HIV-positive men and women in Africa. For the last few years, more women have become infected than men, and in some parts of Africa there are six HIV-positive women for every HIV-positive man. This phenomenon is due to the fact that women are having sexual relations at ever younger ages, and with men older than they. Their risk of infection thus increases, since their mucous membranes are more fragile than those of older women.

The third phase began in the mid-1980s, and has affected Asia, Eastern Europe, and the Middle East. It now appears that the epidemic will be very significant in Southeast Asia, India, China and Austral Africa, based on its rapid spread in the last ten years, the population density, and the very high rate of latent tuberculosis among the populations of these countries. We have already seen in Africa how seriously tuberculosis aggravates HIV infection.

The gravity of the epidemic and its rapid spread across the

world raise the question of whether it might not have already reached its peak. In all epidemics that humans have had trouble controlling, the explosive beginnings were followed by a leveling-out or stationary phase, which was then followed, after varying amounts of time, by a descending curve as resistant individuals are selected and less virulent strains of the germ appear. As concerns AIDS, we are still in the ascending phase. We still cannot tell when it will stabilize on its own, barring any human intervention. On the other hand, we do have, much more than in the past, the possibility of affecting its development, thanks to the knowledge we have acquired and disseminated about the disease, to the medical solutions taking shape, and to the means of communication that make their implementation possible.

I must concur with the directors of the World Health Organization that the epidemic cannot be stopped until a global prevention policy is implemented and an effective vaccine made available to all, especially the third world.

III

TREATMENT

5

Living with the Virus

⤳ *DIVISION* of labor is the rule in the field of medical research. Clinicians take care of the sick, whom they often consider their property. Researchers take care of lab work. And most importantly, no one can stray from his or her corner. I have taken the risk of transgressing these customs, for I feel that in order to advance in the struggle against this complex disease of AIDS, it is essential that patient, clinician, and researcher work closely with one another. The ideal would be for the physician by day to be a researcher by night, or vice versa. I am far from that; on the other hand, my medical training has been of great use to me.

Moreover, we have numerous HIV-positive people helping us in our research, some for more than ten years. I have always personally followed their cases along with the clinicians who are medically responsible for them. I am particularly grateful to those patients who have generously agreed to participate in our research projects. They tell us about themselves and give us their blood; for our part, we try to explain our goals, projects, and perspectives. Thanks to them, I have learned that HIV is a viral infection unlike all the others. First of all, it is certainly the first disease about which certain patients know as much as their doctors do. Secondly, since its evolution is slow, problems of medical, social and psychological care arise over the course of time; hospitals (the medical establishment) as well as society at large have realized that the situation calls for a coordinated interdisciplinary approach to the patient, one that takes into account his or her living situation. Eventually, this new approach will extend to all chronic human illnesses, including cancer, degenerative diseases, and autoimmune diseases (such as multiple sclerosis).

Over the years at least in developed countries, a comprehensive approach to medical and social problems has taken palce. Patients have assumed active roles in this process, through associations that very often have been the first to recognize their own needs, becoming their mouthpieces and responding to demands on both the local and individual levels in collaboration with public authorities. They have come a long way in terms of taking charge of HIV-positive people. Many problems still remain, however, especially questions of confidentiality and access to care.

Today pneumocystosis is still very often the sign that one has entered the disease stage, and in many cases it occurs in patients who have been diagnosed but not monitored; if they had been, an antibiotic treatment could have effectively prevented the onset of the illness.

"What is the point of knowing I am HIV-positive?" ask many people who have every reason to believe they might be infected. It is better, they think, to act as if nothing is any longer of any importance. What is the point of going to see doctors, when medicine is helpless against the disease anyway?

Clearly, it is not only the spread of the epidemic, the virus itself, and the onset of illness that we must fight against, but also such attitudes as these, which are born of despondency and despair.

Learning of a Positive HIV Test Result

Your world comes tumbling down. All that you had believed in, that gave meaning to your life, your plans, is suddenly called into question by a single word written in your test results or uttered by a doctor: "positive." You lose your bearings, are invaded by a feeling of dread. "Why me? When did this happen? Who infected me? What am I going to do?" Calmly, and perhaps with a bit of embarrassment, the doctor explains that you must inform your sexual partners and urge them to be tested as well, that you must not despair because progress is being made, and that you will have to be monitored now. But you are not listening. What is the point, anyway? In such a state of confusion, how can you not feel as though your life is threatened? "I want to be alone, I want to go away. Nobody can understand. Nobody can help me." And the voice in front of you continues: You must use condoms, lead a normal life, seek consultations at a specialized center, stop shooting up. And once outside, in the street, you realize the word "AIDS" has barely even been uttered, if at all. But it invades your thoughts just the same: "I have AIDS . . . I have AIDS . . ." And you want to scream, to spit in the faces of the passersby. And you feel more alone than ever before.

This shock begins a very critical period, one of doubt, self-absorption, disgust, even shame. "I didn't talk to anyone about it. I was afraid my lover would leave me. I didn't tell my parents either: I didn't want to make them suffer, and I felt ashamed. For three weeks I saw no one at all. At work I tried to be as normal as possible. Finally I broke down and told my lover. We cried together." Apparently nothing has changed. At this point you can keep deceiving yourself, denying the disease that is lying in wait; you can even abandon oneself to the very behaviors that favored infection in the first place. "It's hopeless, so I carry on as before."

A certain amount of time passes before your new life as an HIV-positive person can begin. Little by little, rituals are established: Examinations and doctors' appointments begin to form a cadence over the following weeks and months. Medications begin more and more to invade your home life. Above all, your perceptions of yourself and others change. Learning of your seropositive status was certainly a shock. But it is only now, with these gradual, insidious changes in your lifestyle, that the real break with the past occurs. A rearrangement, material and symbolic, of your very existence becomes a necessity. Everyday life must be conceived and organized in another fashion, work and relationships with others reconsidered. And all the while, fear of the disease and of rejection lurks deep inside, along with the ever more insistent questions: Whom should I tell? Whom should I not tell?

It is important to have sympathetic listeners: loved ones, of course, but the doctor too. Such an outlet will always be necessary, because living with the disease inevitably brings moments of despair and reassurance, fear and comfort, desire and revolt, and loneliness. Most important of all is the need not shut oneself up in this looming illness, which for the present the HIV-positive person experiences only as an idea. The patient must agree—perhaps after a moment of refusal—to continue seeing to his or her doctor. The patient's psychological balance and physiological condition both depend on doing so.

"A number of already socially vulnerable people, when they learn they are HIV-positive—and because of the way they learn it, slam-bang, without precise details—flee the health-care system and take an indefinite amount of time to seek help," says a doctor from one AIDS association. "For lack of any follow-up," says another, "people come to us sick and wasted, and at the very edge of the edge where they already were before becoming HIV-positive. There can be no more bodily comfort for them; sometimes it is too late to do anything but help them die in decent conditions, with as little suffering as possible, and most importantly to open a dialogue, as human dignity demands."

The Doctor-Patient Relationship

The most important aspect of follow-up care is establishing a relationship of trust between the infected person and your doctor. The quality of emotional rapport and psychological support, the accuracy of the information given, the changes suggested—these are every bit as important as the purely medical aspects of the relationship.

The general practitioner is on the front line, informing, urging detection, and reporting his or her findings. The general practitioner will also serve as a point of reference throughout the long history of the illness that is just now beginning for the newly informed patient. With the advice the general practitioner gives through regular monitoring, he or she becomes the link and preferred intermediary between patient and hospital.

The response of general practitioners to HIV infection has been rather mixed. In the early 1980s some sprang into action immediately and were behind the creation of support organizations for the infected. Well-informed, sometimes as well as the best hospital specialists, these support organizations play an important role as liaisons in spreading information and putting pressure on the authorities.

This trend has been reinforced by the creation of doctor/hospital networks that bring together private practitioners and hospital physicians of every specialization willing to devote themselves to caring for HIV patients. The general practitioners go into the AIDS clinics of the hospitals to enrich their understanding of the infection and regularly attend meetings, pursuing an ongoing education that gives them the opportunity to exchange ideas and share their knowledge. These networks thus make it possible for patients to be cared for in the hospitals and privately by the same teams of physicians.

The doctor must be able to accompany the patient and patient's loved ones throughout the course of the illness, while guaranteeing confidentiality. This aspect may lead to some tough dilemmas for the physician. For example, depending on local laws, the doctor may not have the right to inform the spouse or partners of a patient's HIV-positive status. Once seropositivity has been verified, however, the physician must urge the patient to warn present and past partners, so they too can be tested and take the necessary precautions. For psychological reasons, some HIV-positive people cannot bear to take this step. As one patient said, "I am bisexual, I adore my wife and occasionaly have relations with a boyfriend. When I learned I was HIV-positive, I was able to tell my friend a few months later, but I didn't tell my wife anything. I have intercourse less and less often with her and always use condoms now. She doesn't understand why. I tell her it's for fear of sexually transmissible diseases. I have spoken about it to my doctor. But I don't know if I'll ever be able to tell her. I am very uneasy about this; I don't think she would understand; she would reject me." This is precisely the sort of situation in which the doctor's role in improving communication and understanding is of fundamental importance.

A certain tension may follow, which may lead the patient to leave his doctor. In this instance it becomes very difficult to ascertain whether or not the HIV-positive has informed his or her partner, and very awkward for the doctor to remain silent, especially when, for example, the patient's partner is pregnant and worried. The doctor is then caught between two contradictory obligations: respecting medical confidentiality and doing everything within his or her power to prevent infection. Only a relationship of the greatest mutual trust can overcome such difficulties. The day we have a treatment for HIV-positives capable of eradicating the virus and stopping infection, these principles of confidentiality and nonobligatory screening can be reconsidered. For now, however, only dialogue combining gentle persuasion and understanding can be brought to bear on the patient.

EVERYDAY LIFE

HIV is a very fragile virus that can only be transmitted through sexual relations and the blood. AIDS is not contagious. Everyday actions and objects should not be cause for discrimination or fear. The HIV-positive person and his or her loved ones may share tableware and bed linens, and these can be washed in the same machines. There is no need to disinfect the sink, the dishes, bathtub, toilets, for which the rules of normal hygiene are sufficient. Only razors and toothbrushes should remain strictly personal, on account of the risks of cuts and small sores one can get on the skin or the gums. But it is pointless to increase precautions disproportionately: they would only serve to add to the anxiety of the HIV-positive person and his loved ones.

An HIV-positive person should not keep getting exposed to the virus by having unprotected sexual relations with other HIV-positive people or by exchanging needles. No studies have proved the role of repeated HIV infection in accelerating the process of the disease; however, it is advisable to avoid it.

Certain narcotics, particularly opium derivatives, weaken

the immune system. Addicts should therefore make every effort to stop taking drugs, or if that is impossible, to join a methadone substitution program. Unfortunately many drug users, upon learning they are HIV-positive, find it harder than ever to wean themselves of their habits.

Alcohol and tobacco, for their part—at least *in vitro*—favor HIV replication. Studies on humans are hard to evaluate, but in any case it is best to cease consumption of these substances, or failing this, to moderate it.

The point is not for physicians to say peremptorily to their patients, "No more sex, no more drugs, no more cigarettes, no more alcohol," but rather to adapt these notions to each individual. In a general way, it is best to avoid excess of any sort. The support and discussion groups that have been set up in the associations are particularly useful, because they allow everyone to express themselves and to exchange their experiences with others also living with the virus.

Nutrition is also of critical importance. The patient must be very attentive to the quantitative and qualitative balance of his or her diet. The daily intake of proteins must be sufficient to prevent the muscles from atrophying; one must also not forget vitamins and trace elements. The doctor may sometimes have to supplement nutrition once the asymptomatic phase begins. Some researchers have found indications of hypermetabolism occurring during resting periods—that is, greater energy consumption during rest than in normally healthy people. One must therefore eat more, and better. This enables the patient to maintain normal weight for as long as possible and to prevent the establishment of a vicious cycle of anorexia, depression, immune deficiency, and atrophy of the intestinal villi (the pocketlike linings where absorption of nutrients occurs). Emaciation not only has physical consequences: it also has a psychological impact on the patient, who feels more ill the thinner he or she gets, and on those around the patient, who soon can only see him or her as a sick person.

By the same token, morale is very important. It is not easy to state exactly what the connections are between stress and the immune system, but there have been many cases where notification of an infection, the death of a loved one, or a bout of depression, have caused a sharp drop in T4 lymphocytes. It is therefore essential for the patient to be surrounded by caring persons, to have a trusting relationship with a few loved ones and with one's doctor, and to have access to psychological and psychiatric care if necessary.

TREATMENT

The most important decision concerns whether to prescribe triple-drug therapy, or (in the clinician's jargon) highly active antiretroviral therapy (HAART). This decision is proposed by the doctor, but ultimately has to be made by the patient on the basis of the information given by the doctor and laboratory tests.

If the infection is very recent, the treatment should start as soon as possible. Since the first weeks are critical for the future course of the disease, it is essential to keep the initial viral load as low as possible.

But if the patient has passed this phase and shown no clinical signs during the first weeks of infection, and if the viral load is low and the number of T4 lymphocytes is still high, then the decision is more difficult. Often it is preferable to start dual-drug therapy with reverse transcriptase inhibitors, keeping HAART for when the viral load is high and the T4 number is dropping rapidly, which occurs just before entering the clinical AIDS phase.

It is a remarkable fact that triple-drug therapy has completely changed the lives of HIV-infected persons. By drastically reducing the episodes of opportunistic infections and partly restoring the immune system, it allows the HIV-infected person to return to an almost normal life, avoiding long hospital stays.

However, the drug regimen is very strict, and patient compliance must be rigorous. Some drugs must be taken during meals; this is the case with AZT and 3TC (lamivudine), often now combined in the same pill. By contrast, ddI (didanosine), which is destroyed by stomach acids, has to be taken between meals. The regimen is still more drastic for protease inhibitors. Indinavir has to be taken three times a day, with a cup of tea or a glass of water but no food. Since the drug is concentrated by the kidneys, it can easily precipitate there as crystals, giving rise to massive kidney stones. It is therefore necessary to take at least two liters of water every day. Ritonavir, on the other hand, has to be taken during meals. Saquinavir has poor bioavailability (concentration in the blood). However, when associated with ritonavir, which blocks some liver enzymes (P450 in particular) and increases saquinavir's concentration in the blood, saquinavir becomes much more potent.

Each of these products, and others more recently made available such as d4T (stavudine) and nelfinavir, can induce side effects that sometimes make them intolerable to the patient and oblige the doctor to try alternatives. Among the side effects are anemia (with AZT); effects on peripheral nerves, such as pain and paralysis (with ddI and d4T); and nausea, diarrhea, and digestive or skin intolerance (with all of these drugs).

In most cases the patient learns how to best adjust to the treatment and to respect the everyday rules, which then become a routine. And the special benefits of adhering to the regimen are that within a few weeks the fatigue and other infection problems associated with HIV diminish or even disappear, and the viral load in the blood becomes undetectable! The patient then becomes fixated on the regular counts of his or her viral load and T4-cell numbers (made every two or three months)—happy when the viral load is low, anxious when it becomes high again.

And unfortunately the worst is eventually likely to happen: the virus continues to replicate in some less accessible reservoirs of the body and generates mutants which are resistant to the triple-drug combination. The doctor then has to try other antiviral drugs, but cross-resistances are frequent: a strain of the virus resistant to a drug already used may also be resistant to another drug not yet tried. These resistances occur quickly and frequently when compliance is not fully adhered to: if the patient interrupts treatment for even a few days, the virus comes back and replicates intensively, generating more resistant mutants.

Since compliance depends on a good relationship between patient and doctor, the psychological support given by the latter is critically important.

However, compliance is not the sole problem. Even when patients respect strict observance for six months, one year, two years, it is difficult to foresee continuing—for five, ten, even twenty years—a treatment that is so expensive for society and so damaging for the patient. This is because new secondary effects appear. The long-term use of protease inhibitors in particular leads to drastic changes in lipid metabolism, which result in the movement of fatty mass (toward shoulders and abdomen), and very high plasma levels of triglycerides and cholesterol, which can result in atherosclerosis and heart disease.

We are still in the infancy of antiviral treatment for HIV and AIDS. It resembles the early days of treatment of tuberculous meningitis by streptomycin: the patient was cured of tuberculosis, the life was saved, but often at the price of an irreversible deafness.

One should never forget that AIDS is still a formidable, life-endangering disease. It would be foolhardy to drop the behaviors of prevention and chance becoming infected, counting on an improbable cure.

A Changing Relationship between the Medical Establishment and the Patient

A long and complex illness, AIDS has put the spotlight on hygienic and social developments of the last few decades. All the new advances in the last couple of decades in the field of science led to making medicine more compartmentalized, specialized, and technical. The patient was in danger of becoming merely an object of scientific interest. It was only with the arrival of this disease, and with the collective awareness that it spawned, that a certain misdirection in our society has become apparent. In amending this misdirection, we should of course preserve the finest medical technology, but we must also take into account the human being, his or her distress, pain, and loneliness in the face of the disease. The approach should be a total one: all the parameters of the infection and all the components of life should be taken into account, so that, in the absence of a cure, we may at least provide AIDS patients with a better life.

Fortunately, new relationships have been established between doctors and their patients. Most HIV-positive people and AIDS patients are young. They are often as well informed about their illness as their doctors and competently follow the scientific literature on the disease. This new kind of interaction is fundamental and marks an irreversible change in health care. The patient becomes an important player in managing his or her illness, a shift that will soon extend to other chronic illnesses that medicine has not yet defeated. The same relationship is true of the associations, which in demonstrating their capacity for innovation, their efficiency, and their spirit of solidarity have henceforth assumed an important place in the health-care system of developed countries.

6

Treatments:

History and Perspectives

ᵔ *At* present no treatment exists that will eradicate HIV infection and allow the patient to fully recover from AIDS. However, after much uncertainty, researchers and clinicians have made great strides toward turning AIDS into a chronic, treatable, and perhaps one day curable, disease.

When AIDS first appeared, doctors found themselves powerless. The discovery of the virus aroused the hope that we might be able to combat it with the few known antiretroviral molecules with which we already had clinical experience. Indeed, during the 1970s, some of these had been used without success in treating certain forms of leukemia that, it was thought, might be associated in certain cases with retroviral infections. By 1984 we had tested their effectiveness in AIDS patients. At the time, Jean-Claude Chermann was working on a mineral molecule called HPA23 and had demonstrated its effectiveness on reverse transcriptase. At the Pasteur Institute, we also had clinical experience of the use of this product in treating Creutzfeldt-Jakob disease, a degenerative brain disorder related to mad cow disease and thought to be caused by prions. HPA23 was given to patients suffering from AIDS, to young hemophiliacs in particular. Unfortunately, this molecule and a good number of others did not reproduce *in vivo* the same antiretroviral activity they had demonstrated *in vitro*.

Meanwhile, rapid testing made it possible to evaluate in record time the ability of thousands of molecules already synthesized by the big pharmaceutical laboratories to inhibit viral production. This was how Hiroaki Mitsuaya and his colleagues at the National Institutes of Health (NIH), together with researchers at Burroughs Wellcome (now Glaxo Wellcome), discovered the remarkable *in vitro* antiviral effect of a product of the Burroughs Wellcome laboratory with the code name BW 509. It was azidothymidine (AZT) a nucleoside analogue synthesized in 1964. Its antitumor properties had proved mediocre; in addition, this molecule was toxic in animals. It had thus remained on a shelf with many other such products until the day when the laboratory decided to test it for its effect on HIV. Quite remarkably, AZT passed quickly from the laboratory to the first therapeutic tests. But the initial enthusiasm of clinicians was later tempered somewhat. We shall soon see why. Numerous analogous molecules, nucleosides, were then synthesized and tested. Some—such as ddI, ddC, 3TC, and d4T—are in use today, having now been authorized for marketing.

Other approaches have also been tried, such as blocking the cells' receptor to the virus by the use of soluble CD4 and paradoxically administering immune suppressors such as cyclosporin after several days of treatment. Cyclosporin, used for suppressing the rejection of transplanted organs, was initially used in France on some AIDS patients, but unfortunately in the terminal phase. The media sensation that followed this experiment detracted from the interest presented by the fact of treating the autoimmune component and activating the immune system during the course of the illness. This list of approaches and different molecules is far from complete. Even if there are no miracles, hope is plentiful. But to demonstrate a molecule's effectiveness, it is necessary to conduct clinical tests, which become longer and more exacting the more the medication's effect is feeble and difficult to prove.

Thus it is mostly thanks to the work of doctors—to their day-to-day observations, to their collaboration with researchers patients, and pharmaceutical companies—and to international cooperation in clinical tests that, bit by bit, time has been gained in patients' struggles for survival. And it is thanks to our greater knowledge of the mechanisms of the disease that we shall one day succeed in conquering AIDS. The current approach consists of combining several antiviral medications in such a way as to avoid or retard the formation of mutations resistant to these antivirals. A decisive turning point came in 1995–1996, thanks to three independent advances: (1) the confirmation that from the onset of infection and during the silent phase of infection the virus is continuously infecting new cells in the lymphatic tissues; (2) the pharmaceutical industry's development of much more powerful substances—the protease inhibitors—for limiting the infectivity of the virus: and (3) the use of new (surrogate) laboratory markers that make it possible to evaluate precisely through a blood test the quantity of viral multiplication, hence the effect of the treatment, and the verification of the relationship between these markers and the clinical condition of the patient.

The Treatment of Opportunistic Infections

Before going into the details of what would appear to be a revolution for the well-being of HIV-positive people, let us recall that great progress had already been made toward saving or prolonging the lives of infected patients by the curative and preventive treatment of opportunistic infections.

Thirteen years ago, AIDS revealed itself to the world through pneumocystis pneumonia (pneumocystosis), which occurs only in people with depressed immune systems. At the time, it was very rarely diagnosed. Today it is the most common of the opportunistic infections, and the one for which we possess the best preventive courses of action. Two of the other opportunistic infections are Kaposi's sarcoma and lymphomas, which many researchers believe to be viral in origin.

The list of these opportunistic infections was completed over the last ten years. Their appearance during the evolution of AIDS has now come to be appreciated; diagnostic methods have been established, effective treatments formulated. For a good number of these infections, primary and secondary prevention procedures have been developed: primary being aimed at preventing the first infectious episode, secondary at avoiding a possible recurrence.

These treatments have made it possible to postpone the occurrence of these infections and to make life more comfortable for patients by ensuring a longer active social and professional existence. Moreover, the average length of time remaining to full-blown AIDS sufferers has increased from eight months in 1981 to a little less than three years in 1994; because of this increased life expectancy, however, certain pathologies have become more frequent at this late stage of the illness: *Mycobacterium avium* (an infection of the digestive tract), cytomegalovirus (CMV) infection, and esophageal candidiasis (caused by the fungus *Candida albicans*). Effective prevention of some of these infections has decreased their frequency.

When the level of T4 lymphocytes in the blood falls to between 500 and 200 per cubic millimeter, three pathologies often occur. Candidiasis first appears in the mouth; it is easily treated, but relapses may occur. Shingles caused by the varicella-zoster virus is easily treated and prevented after the first episode with acyclovir, an antiviral compound effective against herpes viruses. Leukoplakia of the tongue also sometimes diminishes with acyclovir; its origin would seem to be viral as well (the Epstein-Barr virus).

Tuberculosis represents a rather disturbing element of the current AIDS epidemic. Mycobacterium tuberculosis strains that are resistant to antibiotics are multiplying. Twelve centers of multiresistant tuberculosis have been reported in the hospitals and prisons of New York, Miami, and San Francisco. In New York, in 1991, 33 percent of the strains were resistant to at least one antitubercular drug, and 15 percent were resistant to isoniazid and rifampin, the two medications most effective in the prevention and treatment of tuberculosis. The emergence of these resistant strains is often linked to a course of treatment left unfinished or broken off too soon by the patient.

Beyond the preventive measures of hospital hygiene, a couple of recommendations are given today for the effective prevention of multiresistant tuberculosis: close observance of treatment procedures for active tuberculosis, regardless of duration and the possible appearance of allergic reactions; and the development and propagation of fast methods for finding resistant bacilli and effective antibiotics.

Instructions regarding preventive treatment for tuberculosis are currently under discussion, whereas this is no longer the case for pneumocystosis. The occurrence of this opportunistic infection today attests to an insufficiency in the care and control of patients.

Primary prevention of pneumocystosis is administered when the T4 lymphocyte count falls below 200 per millimeter or represents less than 15 to 20 percent of the total number of lymphocytes. Every patient is unique, so this decision will depend on the specific doctor. Indeed, depending on the severity of the infection, one can begin this prevention if one notices a rapid drop in T4 cells; if the patient is already in the symptomatic phase, with other infections appearing as well; if there is a change in the patient's general condition; or if a lymphoma has emerged. A few years ago, pentamidine sprays were recommended: administered once a month, they deposit their active ingredient into the alveoli of the lungs. Today this treatment is being widely replaced by oral administration of Bactrim, a medication combining two antibiotics.

Toxoplasmosis generally occurs at a more significant level of immune depression than pneumocystosis. It is caused either by a new infection or the reactivation of an old infection. In the latter case, the person has toxoplasmic antibodies in the blood; one must therefore begin primary prevention if this has not already been done for pneumocystosis, since Bactrim appears to be effective against both infections. The significance of primary prevention against toxoplasmosis is not yet as clear as it is for pneumocystosis.

In France, toxoplasmosis affects 15 to 30 percent of AIDS sufferers. Its frequency of occurrence places it just after pneumocystosis, and it recurs in 50 to 80 percent of the cases. Secondary prevention is therefore a matter of course.

Opportunistic infections play a large part in the severity of the illness. The establishment of preventive treatments has thus made it possible to prolong both the asymptomatic and the full-blown AIDS phases. These treatments, however, act on the consequences of the disease, not on the disease itself. Treatments directed at the virus itself are therefore a necessity. Thanks to the antiretroviral combination therapies, these opportunistic infections have become increasingly rare in patients who can afford them. Consequently, many beds in AIDS clinics remain unoccupied, and more patients remain ambulatory and treat themselves at home.

Antiviral Treatments

To multiply, the virus uses three specific enzymes, encoded into its genetic material: reverse transcriptase, integrase and protease. All three are the best targets for chemical inhibitors.

Currently, only the reverse transcriptase inhibitors and protease inhibitors are used in treatment.

Reverse transcriptase, as we have seen, is the key enzyme: as soon as the viral material has entered the cytoplasm, it sets about transcribing the viral RNA—which exists in duplicate—into DNA. Reverse transcriptase works the same way as the polymerases of the cell's RNA and DNA: by adding, in succession, one of the four bases (thymine, cytosine, adenine, or guanine) in a complementary pairing with those of the chain to be transcribed. (When a ribose sugar is added to the base, it becomes a nucleoside, and the name changes to thymidine, cytidine, adenosine, or guanosine, respectively.)

Azidothymidine (AZT)

AZT is very close structurally to one of the normal nucleosides, thymidine. The reverse transcriptase enzyme of the virus will thus be misled into using AZT in place of thymidine, which is normally paired with adenosine on the RNA chain to be transcribed.

But AZT is constructed in such a way that the enzyme cannot later add any additional bases. The synthesis of the DNA chain will therefore stop, halting the entire cycle of viral synthesis.

One question immediately comes to mind: why does AZT not also inhibit cellular polymerases, particularly the polymerase of the chromosomes' DNA? Actually, it does, but only in doses much larger than those needed to work actively against the virus enzyme. The cellular polymerase more sensitive to AZT is that of the mitochondria, the source of chemical energy in our cells. This explains why the side effects of AZT include muscle fatigue and sometimes more serious ailments in the muscles, which are rich in mitochondria, whose energy is used in muscle contractions. AZT also has a particular attraction for bone marrow cells, which are the source of our red blood cells, and thus another of its effects is anemia. Today such side effects are lessened by halving the dosage that was originally used.

AZT has another drawback: to be active (that is, to be used by the reverse transcriptase enzyme), it must receive phosphate molecules (become phosphorylated). The cellular enzyme that adds phosphates is present in sufficient quantities only in strongly activated lymphocytes. These occur in large numbers during the advanced stage of the illness and are the preferred target of the virus. Yet the virus can also infect and replicate in less activated lymphocytes, in which the concentration of phosphorylated AZT is too weak to inhibit the reverse transcriptase. This is one reason why treatment of asymptomatic patients with AZT alone has proved disappointing.

But there are other reasons as well. Since AZT acts only during the phase of reverse transcription, the already infected cells are not at all sensitive to AZT, since the phase of reverse transcriptase has already passed and the viral genes have already been inserted into the cells' chromosomes.

The macrophages, in particular, which have a rather long life span, even when infected, could thus produce considerable amounts of virus, even in the presence of AZT.

The final—and perhaps the most important—drawback in using AZT is that very quickly, forms of the virus appear whose polymerase has mutated and become resistant to the effect of AZT. The change of a single amino acid in the finger-shaped part of the enzyme that attracts the phosphorylated nucleosides, including AZT, is enough to make the enzyme resistant to AZT, thus necessitating AZT doses ten or even a hundred times stronger to inhibit the enzyme.

It is the reverse transcription phase itself that makes the rapid generation of these mutations possible. During the course of copying its RNA chain to make DNA, the enzyme is "misled"—that is, it inserts a nucleoside other than the one complementary to the nucleoside on the chain being copied. In the cytoplasm of the lymphocytes, where reverse transcription takes place, there is often a lack of nucleosides, since most of the nucleosides are reserved in the nucleus for the replication of the chromosomal DNA. This increases the risk of error, which, as mentioned in Chapter 3, occurs in 1 out of every 10,000 bases incorporated. This means that most of the DNA copies (each carrying roughly 9,000 bases) synthesized by the enzyme carry at least one error, one mutation. By way of comparison, the polymerases of the cell DNA make mistakes of this sort only once out of every billion times; they are 100,000 times more reliable than the HIV reverse transcriptase; moreover, they have correction mechanisms that do not exist in the latter.

Despite all these limitations, there is one domain in which AZT, when used alone, has obtained spectacular therapeutic results: in those cases where the virus is transmitted from an infected mother to a newborn child. A French-American study has shown that the rate of transmission could be reduced by three or four times by continually administering AZT daily to the mother for six weeks before childbirth and during childbirth, and daily to the infant after birth.

This is the first time a prophylactic treatment has made it possible to appreciably reduce the rate of infection. This is probably because the dose of the virus transmitted to the infant is small. Such a treatment is now currently used in developed countries.

Unfortunately it is not yet used systematically in the countries of the Southern Hemisphere, where the number of infected pregnant women is greatest.

Other Nucleoside Inhibitors

Discovery of the antiretroviral effect of AZT has spurred the search for analogous inhibitors equal in strength but less toxic.

Thus researchers at the National Cancer Institute have demonstrated the inhibitory properties of other nucleoside analogues on reverse transcriptase, such as ddI (a precursor to ddA, an analogue of deoxyadenosine) and ddC (an analogue of deoxycytosine). These products have been developed by Bristol-Myers Squibb Company and Hoffman–La Roche, respectively. They do not have anemia-producing effects but are nevertheless toxic, causing neurological problems (polyneuritis).

More recently, other, equally active and somewhat less toxic analogues have appeared, such as 3TC, an analogue of cytosine, and d4T, an analogue of thymidine. Others will certainly follow. Yet no clinician today can prescribe the use of these medications alone, or even one following the other. For in the presence of each of these inhibitors, resistant mutations are going to quickly appear. The mutations, however, will not be the same for all the inhibitors. Moreover, a mutation resulting in resistance to one inhibitor will prevent the virus from putting up resistance to another. Thus the importance of using combinations of drugs.

This is particularly true for the combination of AZT and

3TC. Mutations resulting in resistance to 3TC actually make the virus sensitive to AZT. Moreover, they appear to diminish the general capacity of reverse transcriptase to mutate. In 1995, clinical trials demonstrated the superiority of this combination, which produced an increase in T4 lymphocytes, a decrease in viral load, and a greater sense of well-being in patients.

Yet other, more powerful weapons have emerged: the protease inhibitors.

But before discussing this major advance, we must first mention another category of reverse transcriptase inhibitors, the nonnucleoside inhibitors. Unlike the previously mentioned inhibitors, which act by competing with the normal elements of DNA synthesis, nonnucleoside inhibitors attach to the enzyme itself, blocking its active site. This group includes the TIBO inhibitors, first synthesized by the team of Eric De Clercq at the University of Leuven, Belgium, in collaboration with the pharmaceutical company Jansen.

In a test tube, these compounds are very effective against HIV-1 but not against HIV-2 or SIV. In humans, unfortunately, the mutations resistance to these compounds appear even more rapidly than with the nucleoside inhibitors. This characteristic was even used by the team of George Shaw at the University of Alabama to calculate the speed at which the virus renews itself in infected patients!

These inhibitors do, however, retain a useful aspect: they can be used in combination with other classes of inhibitors. They have the advantage of being not very toxic, even in large doses. They are therefore complementary weapons, to be kept in reserve.

Protease Inhibitors

Retroviruses all have a protease synthesized by a gene of the virus, which in the case of HIV is located at the far end of the polymerase gene. The maturation process of the internal proteins of the virus entails successive cuts at precisely determined sites along a long precursor ribbon of proteins. These cuts are carried out by this protease, which, to be active, must be joined to itself in two identical chains. The action of this protease can be compared to an automatic page-cutting machine for books or magazines, where the pages are first printed in all different directions on a great ribbon of paper.

We are indebted to the German researcher, Klaus von der Helm, for being the first to identify the protease of a chicken retrovirus, the Rous sarcoma virus, in the 1970s. This research was of fundamental importance, and illustrates how indispensable basic work is, before one can even think of moving on to therapeutic applications.

The protease of HIV is very specific, in that it recognizes and cuts the protein ribbon only in certain places. Only the cut-up proteins will receive the definitive form that will render them functional as particular enzymes—protease, reverse transcriptase, or integrase—and also as the structural proteins of the central core of the virus. This configuration occurs at the end of the viral multiplication cycle, when the viral particles bud and detach themselves from the cell surface. Through an electron microscope, one can witness this maturation process: the proteins of the p24 core and nucleocapsid break away from the inner face of the viral envelope to form the dense central core, in the shape of a truncated cone, and then combine with RNA of the virus. If this maturation process does not occur, the virus will not be infectious. Immature particles with clear centers are able to attach to T4 lymphocytes and macrophages and to penetrate them, but the reverse transcriptase cannot function.

Ever since identification of this protease, researchers thought it might be a preferred target for chemical inhibitors. For example, as in the case of reverse transcriptase, one could synthesize molecules that were analogous to the viral proteins but which would block the active site of the enzyme.

The search for such inhibitors, entirely empirical at first, soon became systematized thanks to the knowledge of three-dimensional structure of the active enzyme. This made "molecular design" possible: that is, a synthesis of chemical compounds wedging themselves precisely into the hole created by the active site of the enzyme.

Another problem to be resolved was that of bioavailability. In fact, peptide inhibitors can have a very short life in the bloodstream, by becoming either lightly bound to plasma proteins or held up by the liver, or quickly eliminated through the kidneys in urine.

This is why only a few of the many synthetic inhibitors created by the pharmaceutical companies have reached the level of therapeutic effectiveness in humans. Thus between 1993 and 1995, we witnessed the emergence of saquinavir by Hoffman–La Roche, ritonavir by Abbott, and indinavir (Crixivan) by Merck, with the first significant results occurring in 1996.

The pleasant surprise with these inhibitors, which are often added as a third medication to two reverse transcriptase inhibitors, is that they are much more effective than the latter against viral multiplication and have much clearer biological effects. In fact, they have enabled different research teams—those of David Ho, director of the Aaron Diamond AIDS Research Center in New York City, and George Shaw at the University of Alabama in particular—to further the study of the kinetics of viral renewal, which is extremely fast (less than two days), even in asymptomatic patients. Inhibitors such as Ritonavir and Indinavir make it possible to reduce the plasma viral load (the amount of virus in the blood) by 100 to 1,000 times, a considerable reduction compared with the effects of AZT and even other multiple therapies. These studies and others on stored samples of patients assembled by the NIH as early as 1985, have considerably reinforced the value of a certain lab test, that of the molecular measurement of the viral load. Thanks to refined molecular techniques one may estimate with much precision the quantity of viral RNA molecules, and therefore of viral particles, present in the blood.

This test is based on different techniques that make it possible to increase considerably the amount of viral nucleic acids; one of these methods is the earlier-mentioned polymerase chain reaction (PCR), discovered by Cary Mullis (a 1993 Nobel laureate). Beyond its value in estimating the quantity of virus in the bloodstream—which is supposed to reflect the overall quantity of virus in the organism—this test correlates better with the clinical evolution of the disease than does assessing the number of T4 lymphocytes.

We shall later examine its limitations.

The most important finding, as presented in 1996 at the Institute of Human Virology's annual meeting in Washington, D.C., and the Eleventh International AIDS Conference in Vancouver, is that treatments with protease inhibitors used in combination with two nucleoside inhibitors of reverse transcriptase induce clinical remissions. The number of T4 lymphocytes goes up considerably without, however, attaining normal levels. More importantly, the number of opportunistic infections and deaths decreases; the patient's general condition improves, with a return of the appetite, a gain in weight, and a resumption of professional activities.

These spectacular remissions have sparked a great deal of enthusiasm among patients as well as their doctors. We are not dealing with recoveries, however, but only remissions. We do not have enough experience with this treatment yet to know whether the disappearance of viral RNA detectable in the peripheral blood is long-lasting.

On the other hand, it is clear that even after following this triple-drug treatment, residual amounts of virus are always present in its natural sites of multiplication, the lymph glands and tissues. It is true that protease inhibitors have the advantage of preventing the infectious virus from being released by all of the already infected cells—monocytes and lymphocytes—and thus of blocking the infection of new cells. Nevertheless, they have no effect on cells infected in a partially latent manner, in which only certain proteins of the virus are expressed, or in totally latent cells, when all the viral genes are silently "asleep."

Finally, we know that the protease inhibitors already in use do not penetrate, or hardly penetrate, the blood–brain barrier, which gives access to the brain. As a result, the virus can continue to multiply in the brain cells—essentially in macrophages—and cause damage to the neurons. Moreover, the increase in T4 lymphocytes does not necessarily mean a complete return to normalcy for immune system functions. We do not know very well where these lymphocytes come from. Are they the result of a so-called central proliferation, originating in stem cells of the bone marrow with subsequent differentiation in the thymus? That is unlikely. It would appear instead that there has been a peripheral multiplication in the lymphatic tissues, or a change of compartment, with an increase of lymphocytes passing from the lymphoid tissue into the blood. In this case, we cannot rule out the possibility that these cells might not respond effectively to all bacterial, viral, or parasitic attacks, since they may lack part of the repertoire of defenses.

In children infected by their mothers at birth, the immune system seems to have a high capacity for restoration following triple-drug therapy. This can be seen in the return of their thymus to normal size. Conversely, in aged patients reconstitution of the immune system under triple-drug therapy is limited.

Clearly, the efficacy of such a treatment depends on many factors, but is seems that the earlier it is given, the better, before the virus causes irreversible damage to the immune system.

THE FUTURE

Until now, attempts to eradicate the virus infection, even after administering early treatment, have failed. Therefore, despite significant victories, the therapeutic battle is not over. More than ever, basic and clinical research is needed to promote and bring about the recovery of infected patients. This dream may one day become a reality.

IV

THE FUTURE OF AIDS

7

New Frontiers of Research

INFECTIOUS COFACTORS

IF we are to combat the transmission of the disease and produce effective treatments, it is very important to know whether the virus acts alone or with accomplices—in other words, whether there are any cofactors that heighten its effect.

I first asked myself this question in 1983, and I am still asking myself the same thing today. Indeed, the origin of the epidemic remains a mystery, and the virus seems older than the epidemic. Moreover, the difference in the rates of heterosexual transmission between countries of the Northern Hemisphere and those of the Southern Hemisphere needs explanation. So does the long asymptomatic period between the time of primary infection and the onset of the clinical illness, a phase whose duration greatly varies from individual to individual, and which might depend on the interaction of the virus and immune system with infectious cofactors.

As early as 1983, after isolating the virus, we were faced with an obvious paradox: retroviruses, generally speaking, in order to move into a cell, need the cell to be multiplying actively. Indeed, proviral DNA is produced in the cytoplasm by reverse transcriptase action, and in order to become integrated with the cell's DNA, it must pass into the nucleus. This is only possible at the moment of cell division. However, the majority of the immune system's cells are at rest and not multiplying.

As mentioned earlier, we know today that this multiplication is not absolutely necessary as far as the DNA of HIV and other lentiviruses is concerned: HIV's DNA can be conveyed from the cytoplasm to the nucleus even in cells that are not dividing, such as macrophages, and in lymphocytes that are in an activated state not necessarily leading to cell multiplication. On the other hand, when lymphocytes are totally at rest they lack the energy sources required to transport the viral DNA into the nucleus. Instead, it remains in their cytoplasm, where it "dies" on the spot, chewed up by cellular enzymes.

The overwhelming majority of the immune system's lymphocytes, especially those in the bloodstream, are normally at rest. Activated lymphocytes are usually located in the tissues, particularly in the lymph glands. Each lymphocyte constitutes a clone, possessing a specific receptor for a given antigen. We thus have a whole repertoire of T cells capable of reacting to millions of different antigens.

When an antigen—one associated, for example, with a viral or bacterial infection—enters the organism, it is initially assimilated (broken up) by a cell of the macrophage type. This cell then presents this antigen to a T4 lymphocyte possessing the corresponding receptor. This action triggers a cascade of signals that end up activating the lymphocyte: its cytoplasm expands, its nucleus swells, it secretes growth factors and prepares to multiply. Thus a whole generation of lymphocytes is born from one clone, all possessing the same T receptor and effectively responding to the same antigen. These cells in turn activate some specific killer lymphocytes (which have the power to kill cells infected by the microbe or virus) or B lymphocytes (which secrete antibodies). At the same time, however, the T4 lymphocyte becomes a preferred target for the HIV virus.

One can immediately see—it was already our assumption at the Pasteur Institute in 1983—that the more activated lymphocytes there are at the start of the infection, the more lymphocytes the virus will be able to infect and the more lastingly it will be able to install itself in the person. The number of activated lymphocytes itself depends on the severity and number of any concurrent infections. We are all surrounded by germs; our immune systems are in a state of perpetual alert, but to varying degrees.

In tropical regions, the number of germs in circulation is considerable. Cases of chronic latent infection are common: malaria, parasites, fungi, and bacteria. The number of cells in a state of alert is high, and this is probably one reason why HIV has spread more rapidly in the Southern than in the Northern Hemisphere.

We know, moreover, that certain bacterial factors increase the virulence of animal lentiviruses. For example, the virus that causes arthritis and encephalitis in goats, closely related to the Visna virus of sheep, infects herds in France, striking young goats especially hard. When the kids are also suffering from a mycoplasma infection, viral infection leads to fatal pneumonia. Similarly, Rauscher's virus causes fatal leukemia in normally resistant breeds of mice when a mycoplasma is also present.

There, we have said the name: mycoplasma. Let us examine in greater detail the possibility that a newly emerging mycoplasma, or one that had only recently spread, might have favored the epidemic rise of AIDS.

But first, what are mycoplasmas? They are tiny bacteria that have evolved toward greater and lesser degrees of parasitism while losing certain genetic functions. For example, they have lost the gene that codes for the synthesis of a rigid cell wall typical of bacteria. Thus they simply have flexible membranes, analogous to those of our own cells; moreover, their membranes "stick" rather strongly to the membranes of the parasitized cells, which allows them to use the metabolites given off by the cells. They are the size of a large virus (200 to 300 nanometers long) and often elongate into filaments reminiscent of microscopic fungi (hence the name mycoplasma). But they are not viruses, since they still have ribosomes, the apparatus for translating messenger RNA into proteins. Parasitism is not a strict necessity for them, and they can be made to multiply in a rich nutritive medium devoid of cells.

What is their role in human diseases? It is hardly a negligible one: 20 percent of all cases of pneumonia are caused by *Mycoplasma pneumoniae,* while many cases of arthritis, urethritis, and vaginal infections are caused by *Mycoplasma hominis* and *Ureaplasma.* Oftentimes, however, there is no sign of infection and we harbor several different varieties in our mouths and mucous membranes without realizing it. Domestic and farm-bred animals are also heavily infected by mycoplasmas, with more visible harm. This general picture might lead one to think that since mycoplasmas are everywhere, it is not very likely they could be the determinant factor in some new disease. That would be ignoring the fact that rare and new forms have been isolated in patients suffering from AIDS.

As with the history of retroviruses, the discovery of mycoplasmas was fraught with errors. In 1987, a young American of Taiwanese origin, Shi-Lo, described a new species of mycoplasma he claimed to have isolated from a Kaposi's sarcoma (KS): he was actually searching for a new virus as the agent of KS. He extracted the tumor's DNA and made this DNA penetrate some mouse cells, a classic "infectious DNA" experiment. In effect, the cytoplasm of the cells was filled with particles that looked like a large virus; these he called VLA, for "viruslike agent." This VLA seemed to infect other cells *in vitro* and to cause illness in monkeys after six or seven months.

Lo and his associates were working at the Armed Forces Institute, in Washington, D.C. which specializes in pathological anatomy. They analyzed the tissues of dead AIDS patients. Occasionally, Lo's team would find the same VLA in the kidneys and livers of these patients. The first publications on this research appeared in rather obscure journals. Lo was quick to realize his mistake: it was not a virus he was dealing with, but an intracellular mycoplasma. He still believed, however, that it was a new species, and he named it *Mycoplasma incognitus.*

Mycoplasma experts then analyzed the new species and found that it was identical, except for a few details, to *Mycoplasma fermentans,* a rather robust mycoplasma capable of fermenting glucose and arginine but whose pathogenic role is uncertain.

In the 1960s, William Murphy at the University of Michigan, Ann Arbor, had already found it linked with forms of leukemia in mice and man, and had postulated it might be the agent that triggered leukemia by inducing an abnormal proliferation of lymphocytes. But then retroviruses supplanted mycoplasmas in the minds of researchers, and nobody talked about this theory anymore.

An entirely different approach led my laboratory to become interested in the role of mycoplasmas in AIDS. In 1987, the Pasteur Institute began a collaboration with the Rhône-Poulenc pharmaceutical company to search for new drugs effective against HIV. We developed a simple test for screening potentially effective products based on inhibiting the "killer" effect of the virus on human tumor cells, the same cells that had been used to produce the virus en masse for diagnostic tests. When the cells were not killed, it was because the product tested had

had an effect on the virus. This test made it possible to analyze, at random, several thousand products synthesized by Rhône-Poulenc or submitted to the company, at the rate of 100 to 200 per week.

One day a professor from Madrid sent in a number of products similar to a known antibiotic group, the tetracyclines. These products proved effective in inhibiting the virus's killer effect. Further analysis, however, showed that actual multiplication of the virus had not been inhibited. In fact, since the infected cells were not killed, they produced more virus.

Commercial tetracyclines had the same effect, which led us to suppose that it was their antibiotic effect we were witnessing. Antibiotics have no effect on viruses; they only work on bacteria. This led me to believe that this effect might be due to an inhibition of the mycoplasmas infecting the cell line being used in the test. And indeed, the Rhône-Poulenc/Pasteur team showed that the line was infected by one or two species of mycoplasma, and that a kind of synergy was occurring between the virus and the mycoplasma to kill the cells swiftly.

The next question that arose was whether the same synergy occurred in infected patients, and whether it played a role in the worsening of their conditions. Were there new species of mycoplasma, or proliferations of existing species, in AIDS patients? Would treating the patient with tetracycline, an antibiotic well known for its effectiveness against mycoplasmas, improve a patient's clinical status?

In 1989, with the help of a few experienced and enthusiastic associates, I launched a whole research program to address these questions, which elicited astonishment in some and skepticism, and even sarcasm, in many of my colleagues. But to the latter treatment, I had certainly grown accustomed by now. As with Lo, this research created much hope, then disappointment, then hope once again. We tried simultaneously to explore the virus–mycoplasma relationship in cultured cells, to develop tests for detecting mycoplasmas in patients' lymphocytes, and to determine whether an antimycoplasma treatment might have any effect on AIDS.

At the same time, Lo and his associates continued their research and ended up isolating, from HIV-positive homosexual men, a new and truly hitherto unknown species, which they named *Mycoplasma penetrans*. The mycoplasma owes its name to the fact that it has the power to invade cells, to penetrate their cytoplasm like a virus instead of living calmly on their surface. This characteristic is shared by two species that we have isolated from patients' lymphocytes: *Mycoplasma pirum* and *Mycoplasma fermentans*. This time we did not find any correlation between infection by these two germs and AIDS, nor did the few other teams studying *Mycoplasma fermentans*.

On the other hand, Lo was the first to show that a significant proportion (40 percent) of subjects infected with HIV—mostly homosexuals—had antibodies specific to *Mycoplasma penetrans*, which meant they were considerably infected with this mycoplasma, whereas this was not the case with the HIV-negative population. We essentially confirmed these findings, and also showed that nonhomosexual HIV-positive patients were likewise infected with this mycoplasma and had antibodies for it.

As for the trials for antibiotic treatments, they yielded mixed results: some patients immediately improved, others did not. We now know that a treatment of this sort cannot eradicate a mycoplasma infection in immunodepressed patients. Antibiotics are cytostatic; that is, as long as they are present, they prevent mycoplasmas from multiplying but do not kill them. And, as with the virus and AZT, variants resistant to antibiotics inevitably begin to appear. In fact, as with other infections, if the immune system is incapable of finishing the job, antibiotics are not enough in themselves to fully eliminate a mycoplasma infection.

Moreover, an isolated antibiotic treatment can even be dangerous. Indeed, if some lymphocytes are doubly infected by the virus and the mycoplasma, a decrease in mycoplasma will diminish the "killer" effect of the virus, and thus infected cells will live longer and produce more virus. Paradoxically, the antibiotic could increase the production of virus. It is therefore always advisable to complement an antibiotic treatment with an antiviral treatment. Today we believe that if mycoplasmas play a part in AIDS, they act in different ways: by inducing inflammatory cytokines such as TNF-alpha (tumor necrosis factor), by abnormally stimulating the T lymphocytes, and above all by inducing oxidative stress through the release of oxidation products extremely noxious to cells. Penetration of the cells by the mycoplasma might well aggravate these effects. The virus may even be "transported" by the mycoplasma. Anything is possible. We do not know yet whether *Mycoplasma penetrans* is indeed *the* cofactor that explains the virulence of HIV, but it does demonstrate the right characteristics: a weak presence in the HIV-negative population, a strong presence in HIV-positives. And there may be still other species of bacteria, as yet unidentified, present in AIDS patients not infected with *Mycoplasma penetrans,* which play an analogous role to this mycoplasma.

The scenario of the AIDS epidemic might therefore be the following: sexual liberation and an increase in multiple partnerships among certain homosexual populations in Western countries led to the spread of a family of mycoplasmas, *Mycoplasma penetrans* first and foremost, from a rectointestinal localization to a genital one, and then to systemic blood infections. Such infections would have gone unnoticed, being easily tolerated, if not for the unexpected arrival of HIV, which was endemic in Africa.

The virus itself, in isolated infections, was relatively well tolerated. But infection with HIV in a subject already infected by the mycoplasma will lead to a considerable spread of the latter, which in turn will favor the multiplication of HIV by increasing lymphocyte activation, cytokine secretion, and oxidative stress. We should note that this hypothesis applies to any agent of opportunistic infection. In the case of mycoplasmas, we are dealing with a silent infection, undetected and neglected, which has perhaps been there longer than the infections usually diagnosed. In this scenario, the AIDS epidemic may have been born of the geographic meeting between the African retrovirus and a germ most likely of American origin, an encounter that may as easily have occurred in New York as in Kinshasa.

The same mysteries, and perhaps the same explanation, exist for past epidemics such as syphilis. The "Naples disease" (as the French called it), or the "French disease" (as everyone else called it), suddenly appeared in Europe after Columbus's expedition in 1492 and then spread explosively through the armies of Europe and the cities they passed through. Blame was laid on a germ imported from America, but syphilitic lesions have recently been discovered on skeletons of Europeans dating back to well before the discovery of the New World. Perhaps here too, what was brought back from America was not *Treponema* (the organism causing syphilis) but a bacterial or viral cofactor that increased its virulence or communicability.

With HIV, it is, of course, quite possible that other cofactors besides some new species of mycoplasma, such as viruses or bacteria, are to blame. Apparently, a virus of the herpes group, called HHV-6, can also potentiate HIV infection *in vitro,* and it is not impossible that this virus—though ubiquitous—proliferates in people infected with HIV. Similarly, another herpes virus, cytomegalovirus (CMV), may also aggravate HIV infection.

All these hypotheses, if they are to be proved, require a long and patient effort at epidemiological correlation. As far as *Mycoplasma penetrans* is concerned, until recently we lacked the proper reagents to determine the presence of this mycoplasma in tissue or blood samples. These reagents are now available.

Most researchers, however, argue against the necessity of cofactors. SIV, a virus analogous to HIV and of African origin, causes AIDS in the macaque, an Asian monkey. Apparently even a virus issued from a molecular clone—that is, from a single DNA molecule—can cause the disease. This would seem to rule out the possibility that a cofactor is absolutely necessary for the virus to have its devastating effect. On the other hand, one could argue that the monkey, in its natural state, may harbor species of mycoplasma similar—if not identical—to those present in humans and which play the same role in relation to the virus. In this case, a massive antibiotic treatment *before* inoculation with the virus, or a mycoplasmic immunization, might slow down the disease.

Obviously these hypotheses are not simply intellectual speculations but could actually lead to the development of vaccines and new therapies. It is a deplorable fact that to this day, the number of researchers interested in this line of investigation worldwide barely exceeds the number of fingers on both hands.

Immunological Phenomena and Apoptosis

A disease of the immune system, AIDS was initially studied by immunologists. It is thanks to the fundamental immunological discovery of monoclonal antibodies, which have exquisite specificity for a single antigen, that we were able understand the characteristics of immunodepression: the drop in the number of T4 lymphocytes and their loss of function. T4 stands for a kind of receptor present on the surface of certain lymphocytes; it is also carried by other cells, such as monocytes, which are equally vulnerable to HIV infection. The T4 receptor is involved in the recognition of the antigen. Researchers now tend to use CD4 and CD8 (CD for "cluster of differentiation") in place of T4 and T8.

Very shortly after first isolating the virus at the Pasteur Institute, we noticed that the virus bound very assiduously to the CD4 molecules, which are in fact its specific receptors.

HIV and related viruses have gone through a long evolution, over the course of which they acquired this particular tropism (a preference for this receptor). It results, no doubt, from some ancient modification, since it is shared by all retrolentiviruses existing in primates. This feature is very useful to the virus, for it enables it to parasitize the cells responsible for organizing the body's defenses against itself.

Three basic principles underlie the functioning of the immune system. First of all, there is the clonal perception of the molecular intruder; for each new foreign molecule (antigen) there is a corresponding T-cell clone for activating the other cells and destroying the cells bearing the antigen, and a B-cell clone responsible for secreting a specific molecule, the antibody, whose role is to bind strongly to the antigen and thus inactivate it or allow it to be destroyed. Then comes the cooperation of the different cell populations, made possible by soluble molecules, the cytokines. And this leads, lastly, to recognition of "self" and "nonself."

How does this distinction work? Some cells are dying at every moment in our body. In dying, they release different molecular products. Why do these molecules not cause the body to generate antibodies or mobilize cytotoxic cells against these "self" products? In fact, this potential does exist. The spe-

cific cellular clones directed against "self" molecules are normally eliminated, mostly in the thymus of the young organism,
or repressed. There are, however, so-called "natural" antibodies that also recognize the self, but they are limited in number
and weak in affinity. It is only in the autoimmune diseases, such
as lupus and polyarthritis, that they present a danger. Indeed,
the immune system is not entirely blind to the molecules of the
self, but considers them a kind of background noise, a shadowy
area that does not disturb its sharp, lightning-fast vision of the
nonself, the intruder.

Our immune system is built for short battles, blitzes of a
sort. It is less prepared for the guerrilla or trench warfare of the
sort that the AIDS virus wages against it. In this case, its reactions can even be harmful and increase the damage wrought by
the virus. As the virus persists, the immune responses begin to
"slip" and the confusion of signals can lead to autoimmune types
of reactions, where the immune cells destroy one another or
the B lymphocytes produce antibodies that vigorously attack
the self's own proteins.

Paradoxically, the discovery of the AIDS virus and the army
of virologists who have since rushed into the breach have
pushed these immunological considerations to the background,
despite their fundamental importance. On the other hand,
there is a mysterious phenomenon that has aroused a great deal
of interest and a variety of explanations.

In 1988, my collaborator Denise Guétard and I carried out
a very simple experiment. We compared the survival of lymphocytes of seropositive patients with that of lymphocytes of
seronegative blood donors in culture medium devoid of activating factors. The lymphocytes of the normal subjects sur-
vived very well for three or four days without multiplying. On
the other hand, the lymphocytes of the HIV-positives, even of
those at an early stage of infection, died very quickly: 15 to 40

percent were dead after three days in culture. Only the addition of a growth factor, interleukin 2, seemed to prevent the culture from dying.

What could have been the cause of this weakness in the lymphocytes? Their death had nothing to do with the virus, not directly at least, for only an infinitesimal fraction of the T4 lymphocytes in the bloodstream (0.1 percent) is infected by the virus during the silent phase of the illness. Moreover, the T8 lymphocytes, which cannot be infected by the virus, also died.

My collaborator, René Olivier, quantified the phenomenon with the use of a laser fluorocytometer (an instrument that counts cells labeled with a fluorescent dye). Another researcher in our laboratory, Marie-Lise Gougeon, and her team then showed that the cells were dying of apoptosis, which was quickly confirmed by other laboratories.

Apoptosis. What does this word, with its elegant Greek resonances, actually mean? It was coined in 1972, by the British team of J. F. R. Kerr, A. H. Willie, and A. R. Currie at Edinburgh, to define the active, programmed death of cells, which occurs like the "leaves that fall from the trees in autumn or the petals that fall from the flower." In addition to "passive" death, or necrosis (where the cell dies from an outside attack), a cell can also "decide" its own death in certain circumstances.

We all engage in apoptosis without knowing it. Thus, in the process of the embryo's formation, in the genesis of its forms, certain cells multiply, but others must die of apoptosis. In the embryo's rudiments (anlages) of a hand, the formation of the fingers is linked to the apoptosis that occurs in the interdigital spaces. Similarly, the cells of the uterine mucous membrane die at the moment of menstruation in women. In the immune system, it is also by apoptosis that the autoreactive cellular clones, those that recognize the proteins of the self, are eliminated in the thymus.

The cellular and molecular processes that lead to apoptosis are only partially known. Several specific enzymes are induced or activated, an endonuclease in particular. This breaks the chromosomal DNA in its least protected areas, that is, between the beads where the DNA coils with basic proteins called histones.

One can observe the various stages of this process with an electron microscope and see the DNA and the histones condense and then leak free from the nucleus. The first part of the process is reversible—the breaks in the DNA can be repaired—but at a certain point the destruction of the DNA becomes irreversible and the cell dies. At the molecular level, a certain number of genes, including some oncogenes, intervene either to trigger or to prevent the process of apoptosis.

Alterations in the expression of these genes can lead to pathological developments. If, for example, genes preventing apoptosis are expressed in greater quantity than usual, the cell produces a line of offspring that will never die of apoptosis: it gives birth to an immortalized line, which may be the beginning of a cancer or leukemia.

But the inverse can also occur. Normal cells, in order to multiply, need to interact with specific circulating molecules called growth factors. If for any reason these factors are lacking when the cell begins to enter a multiplication cycle, the cell triggers its own own death by apoptosis.

What happens in AIDS? When lymphocytes from HIV-positive patients are placed in culture, even those at an early stage such as the moment of seroconversion, a large proportion of cells, T8 as well as T4 cells, very quickly die of apoptosis. This phenomenon can be further increased by stimulating the cells (with bacterial antigens, and ions such as calcium). We have, in fact, developed precise laboratory tests for measuring this effect.

How is this phenomenon related to the disease, and what are its mechanisms? It occurs in all HIV-positive patients at varying stages of illness. We have noted that it is strictly linked to the *in vivo* pathogenic effects of the virus, particularly the decrease in T4 lymphocytes. One finds the same phenomenon, though with less severity, in patients infected with HIV-2. It also occurs in macaques infected with SIV, but not in mangabey monkeys, in which infection has no outward signs, nor in chimpanzees inoculated with the most virulent strains of HIV-1, which, as we have seen, tolerate infection without falling ill.

There can be no doubt about the existence of this phenomenon. The fact that cells die very quickly of apoptosis *in vitro* indicates that they were already "prepared" to die within the patients, and that the process also occurs inside the host organism.

In spite of everything, many researchers working in the field of AIDS, and not the least important among them, have failed to understand this phenomenon or have denied its significance. According to the hard-core virologist, the virus kills the T4 cells it infects, and the whole disease springs from that. This is a naive and simplistic conception that betrays a certain intellectual rigidity or quite simply an ignorance of everything that happens to fall outside one's narrow area of specialization.

In HIV-positive patients, signs of apoptosis are found in the lymph glands, the main focal point for the replication of the virus. It is remarkable that it is not the cells directly infected by the virus that die of apoptosis, but rather the healthy cells surrounding them.

There is an explanation for this paradox: the interaction between the virus's surface glycoprotein (the molecule associated with antibodies) and the CD4 receptor of the uninfected T4 lymphocytes apparently starts a deadly reaction in the cells, triggered when the lymphocytes are activated by an antigen.

This hypothesis was advanced in 1991 by Jean-Claude Ameisen and André Capron at the Pasteur Institute at Lille, and then tested in experiments by other researchers with the help of purified preparations of the viral glycoprotein. Sometimes, in slightly different conditions, these cells do not die of apoptosis but act as though paralyzed, incapable of responding to the activation stimulus and therefore unable to play their part in the immune response. They are said to have become anergic. This process does seem to occur within the body, for at the AIDS stage of the illness, in many patients the CD4 receptors of their lymphocytes are masked by a molecule that very likely is none other than the surface protein of the virus.

Naturally, while this mechanism may explain the apoptosis of the T4 cells, it cannot apply to that of the T8 cells, which do not have a receptor for the virus. Their apoptosis must therefore have another cause.

It might, for example, be explained by the fact that many cells experience a chronic activation that cannot be indefinitely prolonged because of a lack of certain growth factors such as interleukin 2. An apoptosis reaction would thus be triggered in the cells.

In HIV-positive patients, however, the phenomenon affects all lymphocyte populations, including the B lymphocytes. It may therefore have a more general cause and could be related to another phenomenon that so far we have mentioned only briefly: oxidative stress.

OXIDATIVE STRESS

What does this involve? We, and all life on earth before us, learned very long ago to live in an atmosphere that contains a highly toxic and reactive gas: oxygen. Many chemical reactions in our metabolism release or create even more reactive chemical compounds—superoxides, free radicals, atomic oxygen—that can cause irreversible damage to the components of our cells: proteins, lipids, nucleic acids.

Organisms have therefore developed a number of chemical, enzymatic defenses for detoxifying these molecules: we call them antioxidants. We humans have our own antioxidants, but plants are better than we are in this category. They give us vitamins C, E, and A, powerful antioxidants which our bodies are incapable of manufacturing themselves in sufficient quantities.

What happens in patients suffering from AIDS? One notes a significant shortage of antioxidants and a rise in oxidation products: the level of glutathione in the lymphocytes decreases, peroxidized lipids appear in the blood, proteins are also oxidized, and for this reason undergo very rapid enzymatic breakdown. The phenomenon is massive, and occurs at an early stage. Recently the German team of Wulf Dröge observed it likewise in macaques that had just been infected in the laboratory with SIV. The macrophages are an essential source of these oxidation products, which can be lethal to infectious germs.

In addition to the virus, all opportunistic agents can likewise contribute to oxidative stress, and from the very onset of infection, so can mycoplasmas, which notably lack a key enzyme, catalase, which detoxifies certain oxidation products. A mycoplasma infection, even a latent one, can therefore, in conjunction with the virus and other germs, be an important factor in this stress.

We know that the products of this stress can trigger cellular apoptosis. Moreover, one of the genes that blocks apoptosis (*bcl-2*) codes specifically for a protein that reduces oxidative stress. This has led us at the Pasteur Institute to begin tests with antioxidants and to study their effects on apoptosis and on the evolution of the disease. The first results, obtained with *N*-acetylcysteine, a precursor of glutathione, have been encouraging.

Aside from a small number of pioneers—Dröge in Germany and Leonard and Lena Herzenberg in the United States—very few researchers have shown interest in this phenomenon, despite its fundamental role in the illness.

Even if its initial cause is HIV infection, oxidative stress can by itself aggravate the effects of the infection. Thus it should be treated in this light. Of course, many HIV-positive people treat themselves, based on information obtained through hearsay, with antioxidants—vitamins C, E, beta-carotene, and so forth—but they do so blindly and amateurishly. We now have laboratory tests making it possible to measure precisely the different parameters of oxidative stress. These parameters may vary from one patient to another and may change during the course of the illness. They must therefore be regularly measured in each patient and corrective treatments administered as a result. Preliminary findings obtained in collaboration with our colleagues at the Pitié-Salpêtrière Hospital show that an abrupt increase in one of these parameters (peroxidated lipids) occurs just *before* the onset of an opportunistic infection. This finding may make it possible to administer a preventive treatment of the proper antibiotics. It is clear that the study of AIDS requires the collaboration of specialists in many different disciplines.

THE DISCOVERY OF CORECEPTORS ENABLING THE VIRUS TO ENTER CELLS

Since 1985, we have known that the virus attaches itself specifically to the T4 lymphocytes and macrophages through the intermediary of the CD4 receptor itself, to which a part of the surface glycoprotein of the virus affixes itself by strong affinity. But we also knew that this initial contact is not enough to allow the viral particle to penetrate the cells. In fact, certain rodent (mouse) cells given the gene coding for the human CD4 molecule, the virus captured well but without subsequent penetration.

This suggested that other molecules or coreceptors present on the surface of the lymphocytes must also be involved. Many laboratories entered the race to identify these molecules, with varying degrees of success.

In 1993, in our AIDS and Retrovirus Department at the Pasteur Institute, researchers thought they had identified the coreceptor as a molecule present on the surface of activated lymphocytes and endowed with protease activity: CD26. And indeed, there is a decline in T4 lymphocytes expressing specifically the CD26 molecule in patients, even those only recently infected. Yet the hypothesis of CD26 as a coreceptor was not corroborated by other groups, who thus set out in search of other possibilities.

In 1996, the team of E. Berger at the NIH identified a molecule called fusin, which allows the viral envelope to fuse with the cell membrane. But only certain strains of the virus used this coreceptor, the so-called lab strains, which had been isolated from patients with full-blown AIDS—such as the LAI strain, which can quickly kill the cells.

But what about the other strains of the virus, the apparently less virulent ones isolated from people during the asymptomatic phase of their disease? A different direction of research has led to advances in this area. Since 1986, thanks to the work of Bruce Walker and Jay Levy in San Francisco, we have known that the T8 cells of patients infected with HIV could not only kill the T4 cells infected with the virus, but also secrete soluble factors capable of inhibiting the infection of T4 cells by the virus. These factors, however, proved very difficult to identify, because they exist in very small quantities.

In 1995, in Robert Gallo's laboratory at the NIH, Fiorenza Cocchi, Paolo Lusso, and their associates succeeded in characterizing one of these factors, produced in large quantities by T8 cells transformed by the HTLV-I virus. Comparing the sequence of the purified factor with that of known human proteins in a data bank, they were surprised to learn that it belonged to an already known family of proteins, the beta-chemokines. These play an important role in local inflammatory reactions—such as a skin wound—by causing the white polymorphonuclear cells in the bloodstream and lymph to migrate quickly toward the site of the inflammation. Naturally, this discovery does not exhaust the subject, and other natural inhibitors of the virus remain to be identified.

Other researchers have asked themselves the question: Since the chemokines act through the intermediary of specific receptors also present on the surface of lymphocytes, would not these receptors also be used by the virus itself, particularly by the strains that do not use fusin? The inhibitory effect of chemokines might thus be explained by the possibility that they compete with the virus for the same receptors. This assumption has been fully verified by the work of several groups of American researchers among them Nathan Landau.

Indeed, the viral variants which play a role in the early stage of infection seem to use beta-chemokine receptors, especially CCR_5, to penetrate cells. On top of this, it was found that resistance to infection on the part of certain individuals exposed to the virus could sometimes be explained by a mutation that prevented the normal synthesis of this coreceptor. About 1 percent of people of Indo-European ("Caucasian") origin show a deletion mutation in the gene that codes for this receptor. Two copies (alleles) of the gene are normally carried by a pair of chromosomes. The lymphocytes of people who have the deletion on both alleles (homozygous) cannot be infected *in vitro* by viral strains present in asymptomatic patients, usually the strains transmitted through sexual contact.

People who are heterozygous for this mutation (that is, one allele is normal and the other has the deletion) remain vulnerable to infection but may experience a less rapid progression toward the disease. No one of African or Asian origin seems to possess this mutation. Recently, our group identified, again within the Caucasian population, two other mutations on the same gene for CCR5, which also deactivate the receptor.

Why these differences? One would probably have to go back tens of thousands of years in human history, to the moment when small groups of people, previously nomadic, settled down, became sedentary and thus isolated. It is possible that the ancestors of the Europeans were exposed at the time to an immunosuppressive virus using the same coreceptor, perhaps even an HIV virus.

There would appear, therefore, to have been a selection of people who avoided the HIV-like virus, since the deleterious effect of this virus must have exceeded the inconvenience of losing one's functional receptors for chemokines, and since these chemokines can function physiologically by using other molecules, not used by the virus, as receptors.

To make the symmetry perfect, other researchers at the Pasteur Institute and in the United States have shown that fusin, the coreceptor used by the most virulent strains of the virus present in the late stages of the illness, is nothing more than the receptor for another chemokine, called SDFI. They also showed that one could inhibit infection by these strains by saturating the coreceptor with the chemokine itself or with an analogous molecule.

A few mutations in the gene coding for the envelope protein

suffice to make the virus switch its preference from the CCR_5 coreceptor to the fusin receptor (now called $CXCR_4$). This explains why, when probably too many beta-chemokines are secreted, it can so quickly acquire the ability to use fusin, by mutating within the same patient.

In science, happy endings are never so simple as one might hope at first. Here, things have become more complicated as the research has progressed. There are strains of the virus that use neither of these two coreceptors, but other molecules still. It would therefore be very difficult to use a complete range of chemokine analogues, if one wanted to use them as medications. Their therapeutic future is therefore uncertain. Nevertheless, our knowledge of these factors will help us to understand why certain people are resistant to infection, not only genetically but also in an acquired sense, that is, due to a reaction of the immune system to exposure to the virus. I shall return to this matter in Chapter 8.

"DUESBERG"

I did not think, when I first began writing this book, that I would have to explain once again why AIDS is an infectious, communicable disease caused by a retrovirus, HIV. What in 1983 was only a scientific hypothesis shared by ten or so people quickly became the conviction of tens of thousands of researchers, a conviction based on the accumulation of facts.

A few scientists, however, led by Peter Duesberg and Cary Mullis, persist in defending the indefensible—that AIDS is not an infectious disease but the result of aberrant behavior patterns, especially drug use.

Many of my colleagues have already replied, in the most pointed of fashions, to this position. I believe, however, that I too must respond, having myself been called into question, but especially because such a theory can lead to irresponsible behavior and may, as with cancer, prompt patients to seek treatment from charlatans and to find a quick death.

I have known Peter Duesberg since the late 1960s, when we both, independently of each other, were trying to decipher the structure of the nucleic acid of a retrovirus, the Rous sarcoma virus of chicken. Later he provided the first demonstration, using biochemical methods very advanced at the time, that this cancer-causing virus had one extra piece of nucleic acid not present in its non-cancer-causing cousins. This discovery would lead to the isolation of a gene associated with this cancer, the first *sarc* oncogene, which was followed by many others. Oncogenes are cell genes involved in cell multiplication, whose alteration by mutation or a change of position can lead to the transformation of the cell into a potential tumor-producing cell.

An understanding of oncogenes has made it possible to establish a solid molecular foundation for the cancer-forming mechanisms. It was thus with some surprise that I heard Duesberg, at a Denver conference in June 1984, once again call into question the role of oncogenes in cancers, a role he himself had played a large part in establishing.

Five years later, Duesberg backslid again, this time in a domain he knew much less well, that of AIDS, by questioning the viral origin of this syndrome. The questions he raised at the time had already been asked by many—myself first among them—as early as 1983 to 1984; the accumulation of facts, however, had made it possible to answer them. As in a police investigation, it is more often the accumulation of evidence than an eyewitness report that enables one to identify the guilty party.

Duesberg et al. keep claiming that nobody has presented

absolute proof that HIV causes AIDS. And who, of course, would ever voluntarily dare inject himself or someone else with HIV to see if a deadly disease occurred?

The arguments supporting the viral origin are, however, quite numerous. Cited here are those which seem to me the most solid:

1. The syndrome is not an arbitrary aggregation of disparate illnesses but is instead biologically characterized by an overwhelming decline in T4 lymphocytes, accompanied by an extreme depression of the immune system. Thus we have seen the emergence of opportunistic infections and cancers which, though they may of course vary according to the relative prevalence of germs in a given geographic location and climate, are always the same ones: tuberculosis and cryptococcosis predominantly in Africa and Asia, pneumocystosis and toxoplamosis in temperate regions.

2. When a monkey is inoculated (including by rectal and vaginal routes) with the simian virus SIV—certain isolates of which are indistinguishable from HIV-2—a very similar illness occurs: decline in T4 lymphocytes and opportunistic infections, as well as attacks on the brain.

3. Last but not least, antiretroviral treatments (including the very specific inhibitors of the HIV protease) revive the immune system at least partially and significantly decrease the onset of opportunistic infections and death. The effect of these treatments is particularly significant if they are given during the "silent" period of infection, during which the virus keeps on actively replicating. To deny the role of the virus today would be to deny the evidence of the effectiveness of antiviral drugs. It would be a suicidal attitude for an infected person to assume.

How did Peter Duesberg and Cary Mullis ever come to this dead end? I do not question their good faith. I do, however, believe that, lacking a medical education, they did not take into account the complexity of this immunological disease of viral origin, and confused the cofactors (drugs, other infections) with the primary cause. They now seem to be prisoners of the sensationalization by the media, which has helped to immobilize their position. It would be a tribute to their courage and honor to abandon it, in the face of the overwhelming evidence.

8

The Vaccine

"VACCINE" is a magical word, because it calls to mind all the victories over the great infectious diseases. Thousands of times I have been asked: When do you think there will be an AIDS vaccine? Nobody as yet can answer this question, since, despite all the research being conducted in this domain, the problems surrounding HIV are considerable. Nevertheless, scientists have not become discouraged, and research efforts are not lacking. Several vaccines are already being tested on humans. After years of groping and uncertainty, it actually seems that we might reasonably begin to hope again. Of course, the confidence that spurred the beginning of the struggle has yet to return in full; but the pessimism that followed is already no longer in the air.

A vaccine preventively protects the organism from an infectious disease. It makes the immune system "memorize," using antibodies or killer cells, the "scent" of an infectious agent so that if the same germ appears again, the immune system will immediately unleash a protective reaction. A vaccine prevents the development of a new infection; it should not be confused with vaccine therapy, whose goal is to stimulate a failing immune memory in someone already infected.

From Vaccination in General to
HIV in Particular

It was Edward Jenner who, in 1796, saw the benefit that could be gained from the vaccinia virus, which causes cowpox, a benign disease in cows. He had in fact noticed that farmers who milked cows infected with this virus never caught smallpox, a common and much feared illness at the time. By all appearances, contact with vaccinia protected humans from smallpox. Jenner's method consisted of inducing a cellular immune response by scarifying human skin with a preparation of vaccinia virus. It is due to the close similarity between the two viruses that this inoculation also protects against smallpox. In less than two centuries, thanks to the worldwide universalization of this vaccination and the remarkable efforts of the World Health Organization (WHO), smallpox has been eradicated. There is not a single case of it left in the world.

It was Louis Pasteur, however, who in the late nineteenth century, thanks to his vaccines against animal diseases—anthrax, chicken cholera, and above all rabies in humans—laid the scientific foundations for modern vaccination. In homage to Jenner's discovery, he popularized the term "vaccine." With Pasteur began another stage, a century of very fruitful research in the prevention of infectious diseases, in which most of the successes were due to efficient and inexpensive vaccines. Pasteur's rabies vaccine used an inactivated virus in a rather empirical manner. Its peculiarity was that it could be used even after infection, since the rabies virus travels slowly along the nerve fibers on its way to the brain before the onset of illness, allowing the immune system the time to organize an effective response.

The third great stage in the history of vaccination was the

development of two types of vaccines for poliomyelitis, a fearsome disease leading to permanent paralysis and caused by a small RNA virus transmitted through the digestive tract. It was the culture of the polio virus produced in monkey kidney cells by John Enders that made it possible to produce the virus en masse so that a vaccine could be prepared from it. Jonas Salk developed a polio vaccine from killed viruses; for his part, Albert Sabin used a live virus that had been attenuated by serial passaging (generation to generation) in cell cultures.

The principle of vaccination is by now well known and operates the same regardless of the germ in question. The immune system initially recognizes the viral proteins, especially the surface proteins, as foreign. It then unleashes a specific response: the B lymphocytes create antibodies that will attach themselves either to the virus itself, preventing it from infecting healthy cells, or to cells already infected, thus allowing the killer cells, usually T lymphocytes, to destroy them. These specific B and T lymphocytes remain a very long time in the organism and thus constitute the vaccinal memory of this virus. If the organism is then exposed to a virulent form of the virus, these B and T lymphocytes will multiply, secrete antibodies, produce killer cells, and thus stop infection and prevent the onset of illness.

Nowadays there are two major types of vaccine: live-virus vaccines (such as measles, yellow fever, and polio) and killed-virus vaccines (such as flu and polio). In the latter type, the whole virus is lately being replaced more and more by fragments produced through genetic engineering. These are called subunit vaccines. Thus today, the surface protein of the hepatitis B virus is produced by hamster cells or by yeasts in which the corresponding gene has been inserted. These vaccines are safer, because there is no risk they will retain any traces of infectious viruses, as is the case when the whole viruses are chemically inactivated.

The choice of subunits is a delicate matter, because not all the elements of a virus make good targets for the immune system, because it may not be able to detect them. To increase their visibility, they must be linked to adjuvants, agents that increase their immunogenicity.

What form will the AIDS vaccine take? Or should we say vaccines? It is too early to venture a response. Especially since, at our current point of progress, every direction of research must be explored, because the obstacles to the development of a vaccine are many.

Margaret Heckler, Secretary of the U.S. Department of Health and Human Services, was overly optimistic when, in announcing in 1984 the rediscovery of HIV by Robert Gallo's team, she spoke of a vaccine's being developed within a period of two years. HIV is a particular retrovirus for which no precedent existed among vaccines, even among related animal virus vaccines. It is now 1999, and we still do not have a vaccine for HIV.

THE DIFFICULTIES IN DEVELOPING AN HIV VACCINE

The fundamental problem that must be resolved in developing a vaccine for HIV has to do first of all with the retroviral nature of the germ. Retroviruses introduce their genes into the chromosomes of the cells they infect. These genes can then be expressed or remain silent; that is, they can be active or inactive. If they are expressed, the infected cell produces viral particles; it is then recognized by the immune system and destroyed. On the other hand, if these genes are not expressed, the cell remains apparently normal and the virus is not recognized. This explains a major difficulty in eradicating the infection, even at a very early stage.

But this is not the only difficulty. HIV is also highly variable. This variability affects its envelope protein in particular, protein gp120, which enables the virus to attach itself to the cells of the immune system. On this envelope protein there are five highly variable regions whose amino acid sequences vary from one patient to another and within the same patient over the course of time. One of these regions, the V3 loop (so called because it corresponds to the third hypervariable region), is indispensable in allowing the virus to penetrate into the cell. V3 elicits a strong immune response that includes the body's production of neutralizing antibodies, which can inactivate the virus. For this reason, V3 has been used in numerous candidate vaccines. By inducing antibodies that specifically neutralize this key region, researchers hoped to prevent the virus from penetrating the cell. But to escape the highly specific neutralizing antibodies, the virus has only to mutate one of its amino acids, and certainly does not refrain from doing so. More than a thousand different strains of virus, corresponding to two dozen main families, have been registered. Will we therefore need twenty-four vaccines? And what will happen if these twenty-four families become hundreds as the epidemic spreads?

The region of the virus's surface protein that attaches to the CD4 receptor does not vary. It might therefore be a good candidate for inducing the production of neutralizing antibodies. Unfortunately, it is hidden in a pocket in the surface molecule and so is not very visible to the immune system.

The third difficulty in developing an HIV vaccine derives from the fact that it must protect against sexual transmission, which is by far the most prevalent mode of transmission worldwide. Localized immunity in the urogenital region remains a relatively unknown subject, and we have little experience with vaccines creating a response of this sort. Moreover, HIV transmission is carried out not only by the virus itself, but through contact with infected cells, since the virus can pass through cell membranes. Prospective vaccines are only now beginning to take this second possibility into account.

Another difficulty arises from the fact that the virus infects the cells of the immune system, the very cells that are involved in the vaccine response.

Finally, we do not have any good, easy-to-study animal models of the disease. The chimpanzee alone is sensitive to HIV-1, but it becomes seropositive without getting sick. It is therefore an imperfect and very expensive model. Vaccine trials with chimpanzees can only test prevention of infection, not prevention of the illness. The rhesus monkey, for its part, is insensitive to HIV, but SIV, a close relative of HIV-2, produces in the animal an infection and illness similar to human AIDS. The vaccines tested can thus provide information regarding the two steps of infection prevention and slowing down the evolution of the disease, but it is difficult then to extrapolate these findings to humans.

After fifteen years of research efforts, the balance sheet between what works and what does not may seem modest, but we have learned a great deal.

THE DIFFERENT APPROACHES

The fact that a virus was identified as the agent of this infectious disease might have raised hopes for the development of a vaccine via one of the various approaches already tested in this domain. Like all of our colleagues, our team at the Pasteur Institute reviewed what we could expect from a killed virus, an attenuated live virus, the different vectors of subunit vaccines, and liposomes. The first three of these approaches are described immediately below; the fourth later in the chapter.

The use of a killed virus is a classic method tried and proven with other vaccines. The virus is inactivated by a chemical (for example, Formalin or propiolactone) or a photochemical agent (psoralen) before being injected. Unfortunately the immune response in chimpanzees receiving such vaccines was weak, and attempts in macaques have been unsuccessful.

An attenuated live virus replicates sufficiently in the organism to elicit a humoral and cellular immune response. Ronald Desrosiers at the New England Primate Center has observed that macaques previously inoculated with an SIV mutant that was defective in the *nef* gene were protected against infection by the virulent virus. For the moment, however, the analogous situation with HIV—injecting humans with a *nef*-defective strain of HIV—has been made, because of strong objections which we shall discuss further on.

To use a biological agent as vector, a viral gene, such as the one coding for the envelope, is introduced into another virus—cowpox, canary pox, attenuated polio virus, nonpathogenic adenovirus—or into a bacterium such as BCG (bacillus Calmette-Guérin, used as the vaccine against tuberculosis) or shigella (the agent of shigellosis, an intestinal infection). After inoculation with one of these viruses or bacteria, the HIV proteins are synthesized at the same time as the protein or proteins of the carrier agent. The advantage of this method is that it induces a humoral and cellular immune response that can increase protection.

The manufacture of subunit vaccines relies on genetic engineering techniques that enable bacteria, yeasts, or animal cells to produce large quantities of one or more viral proteins. These proteins are then purified and injected into the subject together with an adjuvant to trigger antibodies and a cellular immune response. (An adjuvant is a factor that stimulates the immune system in a nonspecific fashion but still allows it to react better to the antigen being presented to it.) With HIV, it is essentially the envelope protein that has been used. Only the cells of higher organisms are able to manufacture it correctly, in a configuration similar to its natural structure, for it is glycosylated (that is, it carries sugar chains, which makes it more complex). One variant of this approach is to use a fragment of the protein, such as the V3 loop, instead of the whole thing. But since protein fragments are less immunogenic than whole proteins, an adjuvant must be added.

Finally, a new, highly promising approach is also currently being tested: genetic vaccination, which uses naked DNA.

Here is the basic principle: the gene coding for the protein against which we wish to stimulate immunization is introduced into a plasmid, which is a small ring of DNA found in bacteria capable of autonomous replication within a cell, even one from a higher organism, without integrating itself in the chromosomes. The combination is injected into the muscles, which are made up of large, highly differentiated cells that do not multiply.

The messages sent by the DNA will be translated into proteins that are secreted by the muscle cells over a period of months, thus inducing a powerful immune response. The DNA itself seems to be a good adjuvant of immune reaction, which is essentially cellular in origin.

Tests on human subjects have already begun. Some fear, however, that this long-lived DNA may have deleterious long-term effects. It will therefore be a long time before such an approach can be used on children.

THE CURRENT SITUATION

After trials on chimpanzees or macaques, a small number of prospective vaccines have been tested on humans. These are phase I and phase II trials, designed first to verify an absence of

toxicity in the vaccine (phase I) and then to determine its ability to induce an immune response in human volunteers, usually
not at risk of exposure to the virulent virus (phase II).

Yet while there has been an absence of deleterious effects in
these tests, the immune responses obtained have been deemed
too weak or temporary to justify a large-scale trial for efficacy,
called phase III. American and European authorities have, with
good reason, suspended or postponed such projects, which
could have disastrous effects. Such trials would involve thousands of people greatly exposed to the virus, for the most part
in third world areas, and would entail their random division
into two groups: vaccinated and unvaccinated. One can already
see the ethical problems this would create: people believing
themselves to be protected might abandon safe-sex practices,
such as the use of condoms, thus increasing the natural incidence of infection.

One day, however, we will have to "take the plunge."[1] Later
we shall see that there are intermediate steps one can take before embarking on this great, risk-filled adventure. Which paths
are currently the most promising?

Although the solution has yet to emerge, there have been so
many failures, especially in trials on primates, that only a few
approaches are left that deserve to be fully and simultaneously
explored and developed.

The prime-boost-with-live-vector approach: first the immune system is primed with a live vector virus that is harmless
to humans and has been manipulated to express one of the HIV
proteins; then a "boost" is created by injecting a part of this protein. The priming induces mostly cellular immunity, while the
boost induces strong humoral immunity: antibodies, in other
words. After many tests, some large viruses of the pox family
were chosen, the prototype of which is the vaccinia virus,
which was used earlier against smallpox. The smallpox vacci-

nation was very solid, because it induces a strong cellular immune response. The vaccinia virus had a drawback, however, in
that it sometimes causes encephalitis. The testers thus chose
some highly attenuated strains, or even other viruses of the
same family, incapable of replicating in a sustained fashion in
human hosts.

In this way the firm Pasteur Mérieux Connaught came to
choose the so-called canary pox virus, a bird virus that experiences abortive replication in humans but is nevertheless capable after manipulation of expressing HIV proteins,
particularly the envelope protein. The initial injection is then
followed by several injections of short fragments of this same
envelope protein, namely those corresponding to the V3 loop.

Trials performed on human volunteers in France have shown
that most subjects react with a cellular immune response, with
cytotoxic cells destroying the infected cells, and with neutralizing antibodies. A phase II trial on a larger scale is currently
being carried out in the United States under the aegis of the
NIH.

There are still many unknowns surrounding the future of
such a vaccine. Even if it blends different strains of virus, can
it fully guard against the majority of strains in circulation
around the world, since the neutralizing antibodies, especially
those directed against the highly variable V3 loop, are likely to
neutralize only the strains introduced into the vaccine?

Cellular immunity is significant in only a fraction of those
people vaccinated, about 50 percent. Moreover, it does not
seem to last very long and would thus require frequent repeat
vaccinations.

Lastly, nobody can say whether a cellular and humoral immune response is enough to protect against infection. Thus I
shall touch upon some recent developments that highlight the
emergence of new parameters of protection.

The Correlates of Protection

These have come to light in studies with primates as well as with human subjects.

In Primates.

A British group has succeeded in protecting macaques by injecting a vector expressing the SIV envelope protein directly into the lymph glands nearest the site of natural infection (that is, around the genital or anal mucous membranes). Protection was dependent upon a strong secretion of chemokines—those blocking entry of the virus—by the cells of these lymph glands. In a similar fashion, a Dutch group has also protected macaques against infection with a virulent virus by injecting them with the viral surface protein, inserted in detergent micelles. The best correlates of protection have proved to be the secretion of cytokines linked to cellular immunity (interleukin 2, gamma-interferon) and chemokines.

In Humans.

We have long known that certain people, even when exposed repeatedly to the virus—such as through unprotected sexual relations with a seropositive partner—do not become infected and remain seronegative.

We saw in Chapter 7 that in a small percentage of these cases, resistance is linked to a genetic, hereditary factor, a deficiency of coreceptors to the virus. Yet the vast majority of these people have acquired resistance by having "vaccinated" themselves naturally. In fact, most of them have cells capable of secreting large quantities of protective chemokines when they encounter the surface protein of the virus, especially a highly invariable part of one end of this protein. Moreover, a certain number of these people have antibodies localized in their genital areas, antibodies that are secreted by cells of the genital mucous lining but do not pass into the blood. Thus they are not perhaps fully protected, particularly against an intravenous injection of the virus, but they are in fact protected against sexual transmission of the virus.

It is therefore tempting to think that if forms of acquired natural resistance exist, one should be able to reproduce them with the right sort of vaccine. It would have to be administered to the mucous membranes, with an adequate representation of viral proteins, in the form, for example, of lipid micelles (liposomes), but not necessarily to the genital mucous membranes. We know, for example, that a vaccine administered through the nasal mucous lining can induce protection in all the mucous membranes, including the genital ones. The HIV vaccine might therefore be a simple spray, with no need of injections!

As long as it contains the good viral antigens—and this is where the third recent notion comes in.

Most vaccinologists have been concentrating their energies on the viral surface protein, in keeping with successful experiments done in the past with other more conventional viruses such as flu and hepatitis B. The problem is that the areas of the artificially manufactured proteins that induce neutralizing antibodies are highly variable areas from one strain of the virus to another. It has recently been noted that if one preserves the protein in its native form—that is, in the form it has in viral particles (an aggregate of three molecules)—one may induce the production of antibodies that neutralize less variable areas and may, in theory, protect against a greater number of viral strains. Even more promising are the antibodies directed against a particular configuration the molecule assumes after it has already bound itself to the CD4 receptor, that is, at the moment the virus attaches itself to the cell.

Still, there are other viral proteins of importance in an eventual vaccine: those associated with the pathogenic power of the virus, with its ability to cause disease. Two small proteins, aside from the surface protein, stand out from the rest: Nef and Tat.

We have seen that a virus deprived of the *nef* gene could remain infectious in the macaque but with a much diminished virulence, no longer causing AIDS in an adult animal while remaining pathogenic for a newborn. The first weeks of infection seem decisive in explaining these differences. If one analyzes during this period the lymph glands of macaques inoculated with the virus without the *nef* gene, one witnesses a replication of the virus ten to fifty times weaker than of the virus with *nef.*

The *nef*-deprived virus does, however, have the same ability as a whole virus to multiply in cultures of lymphocytes from the same macaques, though activated beforehand. This difference with respect to *in vivo* conditions led me to postulate that Nef's role *in vivo* was to activate the lymphocytes of the lymph glands before they were infected, thus creating a larger number of potential targets for the virus. A corollary of this postulate was that at the moment the virus encounters the immune system, there is only a small number of activated lymphocytes capable of being infected by the virus, a factor that contributes to limiting the multiplication of the virus. This is a very likely scenario, one that has been confirmed in seropositive patients chronically infected with the virus. The slightest activation of the immune system—as caused, for example, by a flu vaccine—increases the viral load, clearly demonstrating that the virus is always searching for activated cells.

But how can Nef activate lymphocytes? Nef is a small protein synthesized very early after the virus has entered the cell and its DNA has been synthesized and integrated. Though at first considered a factor that negatively regulated the multiplication of the virus (*nef* stands for negative factor), many studies have since shown that it is nothing of the sort, and that on the contrary, it is a positive factor that stimulates the synthesis of the virus in the infected cell. *Nef* in fact, has proved to have a variety of functions. For one, it diminishes the recycling of certain surface proteins of the lymphocytes, such as the CD4 receptor to the virus, and some HLA molecules. The virus has probably "invented" *nef* over the course of its evolution, to prevent the infected cell from becoming overworked and dying too quickly from reinfections by the newly reproduced virus, which would limit production of the virus, or to prevent it from being too quickly destroyed by cytotoxic cells.

A second, lesser-known function of Nef is its activity *outside* the cell, when it is turned toward nearby uninfected cells. Indeed, although the protein is attached to the inner face of the cell membrane—turned toward the cytoplasm—one part of its molecule is exposed outside the cell membrane and can therefore act through contact with neighboring cells. It is even likely that some molecules of Nef are secreted and travel at a distance from the infected cell.

Three independent laboratories—including our own—have, moreover, shown that purified Nef preparations, manufactured by genetic engineering from a *nef* gene inserted into bacteria or viruses, can activate dormant or only mildly activated T4 lymphocytes, thus making them capable of multiplying the virus.

The scenario I presented in 1995 is thus as follows:

After entering the organism through the mucous membranes (infection by sexual contact), the virus infects the macrophage-type (dendritic) cells, which then migrate toward the nearest lymph gland. It then infects the sufficiently activated T4 cells present in the gland and multiplies inside them. These cells manufacture the Nef protein that will activate the neighboring cells through a "bystander" effect, or even more distant cells, if the Nef protein circulates. A second burst of viral replication then follows, creating a large enough critical mass to enable the virus subsequently to sustain itself and affect the immune system.

One prediction based on this scenario is that a powerful immune response against Nef—created by inducing the production of antibodies that would neutralize the Nef protein's external effects and of cytotoxic cells that would destroy the infected cells expressing Nef—should protect the organism, perhaps not so much as to prevent infection, but at least to reduce it to the point where it would no longer cause illness. In fact, certain Australian patients who were infected, through transfusion, with a virus with a deficient *nef* gene are free of symptoms more than twelve years after being infected, even though they test positive for the virus.

Moreover, some macaques that had been vaccinated with a vector virus (in this case, vaccinia) expressing *nef* and that produced a cytotoxic cell response against nef proved to be protected against the pathogenicity of a virulent SIV virus.

Finally, in some of our experiments, one macaque that had been immunized by a soluble form of nef and possessed powerful antibodies to it, did not show signs of infection after being injected with a virulent SIV virus.

The scenario imagined for the Nef protein could also be applied to Tat. Aside from its internal effects inside the infected cell (without Tat, the virus cannot properly synthesize its messenger RNAs and proteins), the Tat protein likewise circulates in the bloodstream and can have external effects: that is, it can activate the lymphocytes (although to a lesser degree than Nef proteins), or on the contrary, it can bring about their death by oxidative stress and apoptosis.

Thus Tat is likewise another preferred candidate for a vaccine.

How to Test the Effectiveness of HIV Vaccines?

Among the different forms of trials—the tests on primates (which are indispensable), the first phase I and phase II tests on humans, and the costly, risky efficacy tests—there exists, we think, a new possibility: to test the efficacy of the vaccine by vaccine therapy, that is, as a complementary treatment to antiviral drugs for patients already infected with HIV.

One would do best to choose patients with a high viral load, but whose immune systems have not been completely annihilated by the virus and thus are able to respond to an immunization. The vaccine treatment would thus be added to the antiviral triple-drug therapy, and its effectiveness would be indicated by a more rapid and intense decrease in the viral load measured in the blood.

A positive result might be seen within a few months of treatment, and could be very valuable in encouraging an efficacy trial in seronegative subjects.

Clearly there are good reasons to hope that a safe and effective vaccine will be available within the next decade.

Paradoxically, we are in a moment when some people are wondering if a vaccine is still needed! Their reasoning goes as follows: now, thanks to triple-drug therapy, we are able to save the lives of infected patients, so let's extend this treatment to the entire infected population, and AIDS will disappear without there being any need for a vaccine.

This is faulty reasoning. Current treatments—need we repeat it?—reduce but do not annihilate viral multiplication;
moreover, they do not have access to certain sanctuaries of the
virus, such as the brain. Finally, extending treatments to all the
infected populations of the poorer countries of the world,
while certainly a desirable goal, could only be achieved very
slowly.

Past experience with vaccines for the great infectious diseases, both bacterial and viral, has shown that vaccination is the
most effective, fastest, and least costly means of eradicating an
epidemic, and even of eliminating an infectious agent from the
surface of the earth. Such was the case with smallpox, and it
will soon be the case with polio.

An HIV vaccine is thus an absolute necessity and a goal that
can be attained within a few years if researchers broaden their
efforts and if these efforts are supported by a political will. In
this regard, the declaration by the heads of state of the world's
richest countries, made at President Clinton's initiative on the
occasion of their meeting in Denver in June 1997, is particularly welcome:

> Preventing the transmission of HIV infection and the devel-
> opment of AIDS is an urgent global public health imperative.
> While other prevention and treatment methods must be
> pursued, in the long term the development of safe, accessi-
> ble, and effective vaccines against AIDS holds the best chance
> of limiting and eventually eliminating the threat of this dis-
> ease. We will work to provide the resources necessary to ac-
> celerate AIDS vaccine research, and together will enhance
> international scientific cooperation and collaboration. Co-
> operation among scientists and governments in the devel-
> oped and developing world and international agencies will
> be critical. We call on other states to join us in this endeavor.
> It is my profound hope that this declaration becomes reality.

9
=

AIDS and the World

It's a new world war we must wage, the third one this century. . . .
AIDS is not a destiny; we will not hand it down to the inhabitants of
the 21st century. . . . Let us make our effort truly a war effort. This
requires two means: first, a financial investment equal to the threat,
in all the countries of the world, starting with the richest. And sec-
ondly, we need a coordinated effort from all fields of medical knowl-
edge.

—*Former U.N. Secretary General Boutros* BOUTROS-GHALI,
  December 1, 1993, Sixth World AIDS Day

✦ *AT* the close of 1998, close to 14 million people had died of
AIDS in the world, and over 33 million adults and children
were estimated to be living with HIV infection, 10 percent
more than the year before. Such are the latest figures drawn up
by the World Health Organization (WHO) and the Joint
United Nations Programme on HIV/AIDS (UNAIDS). AIDS
cases across the world break down as follows: 66 percent of
them are in sub-Saharan Africa, 3 percent in the United States,
6 percent in Latin America and the Caribbean islands, 3 percent in Europe, 22 percent in Asia, and less than 1 percent in
Oceania. The predicted catastrophe has become a reality. In
1998, 5.8 million men, women, and children became infected,
which breaks down to about 16,000 new infections per day.
The epidemic has been gaining ground especially in Africa, and
in the last few years, in southern and Southeast Asia. More

Above. *The original team involved in HIV 1 discovery at the Pasteur Institute in 1983.* ❧ Below. *The five young "musketeers" who unraveled the genetic code of HIV in 1984. From left to right: Stuart Cole, Marc Alizon, Simon Wain-Hobson, Olivier Danos, and Pierre Sonigo.*

*bove. Meeting between the author and Robert Gallo in 1986 in New York, when they
*ere awarded the Lasker Prize of Medicine, together with Max Essex. * Below. Symbolic
*andshaking of Essex, Gallo, and the author at Pasteur-Mérieux Headquarters in
*arches, near Paris, in 1987. In the background there is a photograph of Louis Pasteur and
is collaborators, one hundred years earlier.

Left. *The author in his laboratory at the Pasteur Institute, in 1988.*
Below. *The author presenting photographs of the virus to Elizabeth Taylor in 1987, in his lab.*

Right. *The author in the warm room of his lab in 1992, with dozens of flasks containing cultures of the AIDS virus.* ☞ Below. *At the Cent Garde Meeting in Garches, near Paris, in 1990. From left to right: Charles Mérieux, Luc Montagnier, Jonas Salk, and Robert Gallo.*

generally speaking, 95 percent of new AIDS cases worldwide will appear in developing countries, a fact that will not fail to have social, economic, and in the long run, demographic consequences for these countries. The World Bank predicts that life expectancy in sub-Saharan Africa, instead of increasing, will remain the same and even decrease because of HIV. AIDS is going to become a sign and a cause of underdevelopment. For the moment, especially in Asia, most of the people infected are still asymptomatic, and therefore healthy; but we have every reason to believe that they will develop the disease in time. That is when the epidemic will bring the full measure of its devastation to bear. Caring for these millions of people in danger of dying in the coming years will be one of the major challenges of our age.

In the West, AIDS has brought to light the failings of our societies. It has had similar effects in other parts of the world as well: it has made particularly evident the vulnerability of women and the difficulty of caring for the sick in the precarious health systems of developing countries.

THE GEOGRAPHY OF AIDS

Every country, every region has its own AIDS history: it concerns the date of the arrival of the virus and the start of the epidemic, the different patterns of risky behavior that caused its spread, and all the cultural, social, political, and environmental factors that led to its specific spread in that country. Indeed, such factors explain how, in two otherwise comparable countries, the epidemic could spread in different ways.

It is very difficult to present global figures that are totally reliable. The general demographic data are not always sufficiently accurate, or else they are not up to date. In addition, studies are often conducted in limited areas and on specific groups, such as pregnant women, prostitutes, hospitalized people in large cities, and blood donors. They are then extrapolated to the general population, which usually involves a number of inaccuracies.

Nevertheless, it seems that the majority of infections are heterosexual in origin. In North America, western Europe and Australia, the epidemic has been spreading among homosexuals with multiple partners and among intravenous drug users since the late 1970s. Today these groups make up the majority of AIDS sufferers in these countries. The epidemic, meanwhile, is spreading predominantly among heterosexuals, in rampant fashion in the northern half of the world, in explosive fashion in the southern half.

In Latin America, the virus spread in the early 1980s primarily among homosexual and bisexual men and among intravenous drug users. In Mexico, nearly half of the women infected contracted the germ from bisexual men and the rest from blood transfusions. In Brazil, among intravenous drug users the rate of infection has jumped from 20 to 76 percent in just a few years. This subcontinent is now evolving in a manner similar to Africa: heterosexual transmission is predominant and affects women above all.

In sub-Saharan Africa, transmission has always been heterosexual. And while this region holds only 10 percent of the world's population, it has two-thirds of its AIDS victims: 83 percent of all infected women and 90 percent of all infected children live there. Central and eastern Africa are the regions most severely stricken, but it is now in southern Africa that the epidemic is spreading the fastest: in Zambia, Zimbabwe, Swaziland, Botswana, and South Africa in particular. In these countries the epidemic has struck the cities and countrysides with equal ferocity, but always in heterogeneous fashion, like everywhere else in Africa. The rate of infection on the continent ranges from 1 to 20 percent, depending on the country. It is predicted the rate will double in one to three years among the sexually active population in the most infected regions of Africa, whereas it will take five years or more in regions where seroprevalence (number of HIV-positive people) is slight.

In southern and Southeast Asia, the epidemic did not begin until the mid-1980s. It first appeared among intravenous drug users, then prostitutes. Tainted blood donations have also played an important role in certain regions, especially in India. Today the epidemic in India and these regions of Asia is growing along lines similar to Africa, and the potential for spread is all the greater as the subcontinent is much more populous than Africa.

In Eastern Europe and the former Soviet Union, the social and political upheavals of the last few years, particularly the opening of the frontiers, the movements of population, and civil wars, have favored the spread of the epidemic. Here the epidemic has struck mostly homosexuals and intravenous drug users, though there has also been infection through the repeated use of unsterilized needles in the hospitals of Romania and the former Soviet Union.

In eastern Asia and the Pacific, the epidemic has been a fact of life since the mid-1980s, but the data we have on it are incomplete and concern mostly China. Apparently transmission there has been occurring predominantly through intravenous drug use and heterosexual relations. The most recent figures show an alarmingly fast spread of the virus from southern provinces to northwestern China.

For North Africa and the Middle East, we lack well-documented information. Apparently countries under Islamic rule have been less affected than others, even in Africa. However, commerce, drug use, and bisexuality in these countries are factors that favor the spread of the disease and may elude the strictures of religion.

In addition to this great epidemiological disparity between the Western countries on the one hand and the rest of the world on the other, there is also a huge difference in the resources used for health care and the fight against HIV in particular, in the areas of prevention, research, and patient care. The average expenditure for health care per inhabitant is more than $2,000 (U.S. dollars) annually in the industrialized countries, $35 in South America, and $5 or less in southern Asia and sub-Saharan Africa. The average yearly cost of triple-drug therapy ($12,000 per year per patient) far exceeds such figures. It is therefore difficult to imagine any systematic antiviral treatments being administered with these resources, since even the treatment of opportunistic infections such as tuberculosis, which is now a priority, is available in only a limited number of hospitals. Ninety-five percent of the $7 billion spent annually on AIDS in the world is spent in the industrialized countries.

THE SPREAD OF THE EPIDEMIC IN AFRICA

The spread of the epidemic in Africa has called attention to the interaction of political, economic, and social factors that have overwhelmed Africa over the last few years and played a major role in the scourge of AIDS. Political crises, economic development, and the concomitant growth of cities and means of transportation, as well as an increase in seasonal migrations between countries or regions, have favored the spread of the epidemic, which has become endemic.

AIDS appeared in Africa at a moment when the continent was going through several crises, which the disease has aggravated. Over the last thirty years, after a period of economic development, growing problems have led to an impoverishment of many African countries and weakened the social fabric and the family, undermining the basic structures of African society. Migrations and the internationalization of culture have eroded tradition, which until then had played a stabilizing role. Moreover, since gaining independence, a number of countries, such as Uganda, Angola, Mozambique, Ethiopia, and Congo/Zaire, have been weakened and impoverished by political crises. This situation has been further aggravated since the late 1970s by economic crises stemming from drops in the world prices of such raw materials as peanuts and coffee, and from natural calamities such as the drought in the Sahel. These have all led to displacements of population or aggravated the problems already contributing to the destabilization of traditional social systems. Wandering and social insecurity have also contributed to the precarious state of health of significant sectors of the population, creating a favorable ground for the spread of chronic infections and epidemics. The spread of sexually transmissible diseases—especially those causing genital ulcers such as chancroid, syphilis, or herpes, which break the protection provided by the skin or mucous membranes—favors the spread of HIV.

The growth of transportation between the various regions of Africa along the major highway routes has been the cause of some major disparities: the capitals and stopover cities have become reservoirs of HIV. They have the highest and oldest rates of infection: we see this in Abidjan (Ivory Coast), Bujumbura (Burundi), Kigali (Rwanda), and Bangui (Central African Republic). The surrounding countrysides have been less affected, with the exception of those that have sustained relations with these urban areas. For the populations most exposed are those on the move: transporters, truckers, soldiers, seasonal laborers, merchants, and everyone else having contact with them, especially prostitutes. The percentage of HIV-positives often increases the closer one gets to a city. But it is impossible to generalize. Each city has its own history, economic development, customs, and religions—all variables that affect the behavior of its inhabitants and make it hard to generalize. Thus such cities as Lagos, Dar es-Salaam, and Dakar have been proportionally less stricken by the virus than other capitals.

Nevertheless, the concentration of infection in African cities is all the more alarming when we consider that this continent, the least urbanized in the world, has the highest rate of urban demographic growth. The urban population of black Africa, estimated at around 2.5 percent of the entire continent's population in 1920 and 13 percent in 1960, reached 30 percent in 1988. And it was the largest and least equipped cities that attracted the most people in search of work between the 1960s and the 1980s. These new cities, most of which are outside the predominately Islamic regions, are absorbing a great many young, uprooted, single men from rural areas. More recently, unskilled women have also been coming to the cities in search of work. With no resources of their own, some have worked as prostitutes, for lack of alternatives. These migrations, with long periods of separation between reunions, also played a large part in undermining family structures and contributed to the rise in prostitution and sexually transmitted diseases well before the appearance of the AIDS epidemic. When the migrants return home from the cities, they then spread the infections to the countryside.

On the other hand, while urbanization has played a determinant role in certain countries, there are other countries in Africa that are among the least urbanized—such as Uganda, Rwanda, Burundi, and Tanzania—where AIDS has spread considerably. Two countries with particularly high rates of infection serve as good illustrations of how the disease spreads in different ways.

Uganda is one of the most infected countries in Africa: 10

percent of its 17 million inhabitants—or one in five sexually active people—are HIV-positive. Twice as many women as men are infected; among adolescents between the ages of fifteen and nineteen, there are six times as many girls infected as boys. Eighty percent of the transmission is heterosexual, 8 percent is perinatal, 8 percent is from tainted blood. Civil war has broken up families. The economy began to collapse even before 1985, the year of the drop in the world price of coffee, the country's primary export. The recovery plans of many African countries involve considerable austerity programs, which can no longer guarantee even minimum wages for public employees. In such a context, women must do what they can to make sure their children get the food, care, and education they need. Some, to survive, seek out several sexual partners. In addition, certain ritual ceremonies—such as choosing a name for a child, initiation, circumcision, marriage, and burial—sanction sexual promiscuity. These are clearly the most significant factors in the spread of sexually transmissible diseases and AIDS. On the basis of these data, the organization Protecting the Person against AIDS has set up an information program aimed at children between the ages of five and fifteen; they constitute the "window of hope"—children who have eluded perinatal AIDS and have not yet begun to have sexual relations. Active information campaigns on prevention have, however, been fruitful, decreasing the number of new infections in young men.

Ivory Coast is the starting point of a great commercial route in West Africa. Thirty years of peace and prosperity have made it a very attractive center of growth. One third of the population is foreign; they come principally from bordering nations—Burkina Faso, Guinea, Ghana, and Niger—where a great many seasonal laborers quit their villages during the dry season to come and work in Ivory Coast plantations or in the port of

Abidjan. Ivory Coast is an almost obligatory thoroughfare for the bordering nations wedged in by the Abidjan–Ugadugu railway, the rivers, and the roads. As a result, it is one of the most infected countries in West Africa. One Ivory Coast native in twelve is HIV-positive, and this figure is much higher among the prostitutes of Abidjan and the young men, especially military recruits. A recent survey showed that 15 percent of pregnant women in Abidjan are HIV-positive. A 1987 study of the first thirty cases of HIV infection in Niger showed that twenty-six of them had spent time in a coastal country, most often Ivory Coast, where they had come looking for work.

THE SPREAD OF THE EPIDEMIC IN THAILAND AND SOUTHEAST ASIA

The epidemic was late in spreading to Thailand, and did so in a very different manner than in Africa. Nevertheless, after ten years the situation in the two countries is starting to look more and more the same.

HIV infection was first identified in Thailand in 1984. Its first victims were intravenous drug users, then prostitutes and young heterosexual men who subsequently infected their wives. Today the epidemic in Thailand, a more recent arrival than in Africa, is spreading to the general population through heterosexual contact, since it is a common practice for men to have, in addition to their regular mates, other partners with whom they do not systematically use condoms.

Thanks to prevention campaigns, the rate of infection of young male military recruits has decreased in recent years. However, the infection rate for women has not followed the same trend.

One finds the same factors contributing to the spread as in

Africa: widespread sexually transmitted diseases, frequent interactions among groups in the interior of the country—prostitutes, soldiers, displaced populations seeking work. For example, 70,000 Thais left their home villages in 1991 in search of work: women went to the cities and became prostitutes to fulfill the needs of the families they had left behind in rural areas.

THE EPIDEMIC SPREADS TO WOMEN

According to WHO, in the next ten years 7.5 million women will be infected in Africa. According to the U.N. development program, 70 percent of the women now being infected in the world are between the ages of fifteen and twenty-five. Women, especially younger women, are increasingly the prime targets of the disease.

Indeed, their physical constitution makes them more vulnerable to infection than men. During vaginal sex they are much more prone to infection than men, and this vulnerability is greater during adolescence, when the genital tissues are still immature. Men often seek out very young girls, hoping they will not be infected. Thus in Malawi, among adolescents between the ages of fifteen and nineteen, there are five times as many girls infected as boys. In Zimbabwe, a study of the accumulated AIDS cases between 1987 and 1993 shows that among people under the age of nineteen, there was one man infected for every five women. In Nigeria, Kenya, and Sierra Leone, between 16 and 36 percent of all adolescent women have a sexually transmissible disease.

The vulnerability of women also has to do with their social, economic, and psychological dependence on men. They do not have control over their own sexuality and often seek material security from older men. Moreover, in many societies the status of women depends on their being mothers; if sexual relations are protected with condoms to avoid sexually transmissible diseases, the woman will never become pregnant. The woman is not in a position to refuse sexual relations, to demand that a condom be used, or to exercise other options such as chastity, mutual trust, or sex without penetration. Moreover, men in Africa, for example, have multiple partners more commonly than in Europe. Women know beforehand that they cannot prevent this without risking rejection. Thus there is a climate of sexual tolerance. Marriage becomes a risk factor, since women are often infected by husbands who have multiple partners. But whatever the country, prostitution remains fertile ground for the spread of the epidemic. The rise in infection rates is significant, for example, in Nairobi (Kenya): among prostitutes, the rate has jumped from 7 percent in 1980 to 75 percent in 1991. Similarly, in Bombay (India) the rate of infection has risen from 1 percent in 1985 to 29 percent in 1992.

Subservient to men in their sex lives, women have no way of protecting themselves. Without sex education, adolescent women know very little about their bodies, potential illness, and sexuality in general. AIDS prevention must thus involve a major effort to educate women, especially as the problem of children and AIDS is directly linked to their mothers. But it must also involve men.

CHILDREN

Ninety percent of all infected children have contracted the disease from their mothers during pregnancy. The rate of perinatal transmission is higher in Africa (20 to 30 percent) than in Europe (12 to 20 percent). This is probably due to the fact that

African women have to breast-feed their babies to assure them the best nutritional balance possible, even though the virus may be present in the milk, because the risk of malnutrition is even greater than the risk of HIV infection. The threat hanging over the children of Africa is thus a terrible one, especially as they must also face the second consequence of the disease, the danger of being orphaned. It is estimated that at the end of the 1990s, 9 million children will be orphaned. Already 1 million children the world over have lost one or both of their parents to AIDS. Not only do these children suffer from psychological problems, malnutrition, and poverty, but their educational disadvantages and loss of guidance make them more likely to develop risky patterns of behavior. Today in Uganda, 16 percent of the children no longer go to school because of civil war and the AIDS epidemic. One can only imagine the situation in Rwanda.

What can be done for children whose parents are dead? Should they be placed back in their extended families, which seems the best solution but is not always feasible because such families are often already highly destabilized? Or should orphanages be created? The problem should be dealt with before the sick parents die, when the children stop going to school or stop working so they can care for them. Much experience has been gained on the small scale over the last few years, thanks in particular to nongovernmental humanitarian organizations, but such services are in danger of soon being overwhelmed.

THE DANGER OF TUBERCULOSIS

In tropical regions one encounters certain customary signs of AIDS (diarrhea, fever, and weight loss) and opportunistic infections (such as cryptococcosis and cryptosporidiosis) with great frequency, but it is tuberculosis that constitutes the greatest public health problem today: 1.7 billion people have latent infections of *Mycobacterium tuberculosis* (the bacillus that causes tuberculosis), while eight million are actively infected. While the agent of tuberculosis has been known for more than a hundred years and we have effective treatments as well as a vaccine (BCG), which provides relative protection, tuberculosis has never been stamped out in Africa or Southeast Asia. It spreads through the air, carried by the spray ejected from the body when coughing. Simultaneous infection by TB and AIDS is very serious, since HIV infection diminishes the body's cellular immune response, thus helping latent tuberculosis to become active. In its turn, the tuberculosis bacillus activates the HIV-infected cells and creates an immune depression on top of that already induced by HIV.

The tuberculosis epidemic is spreading significantly in sub-Saharan Africa, where TB has become the primary cause of death in adults infected by HIV: 35 percent of the seropositive adults in Ivory Coast have died of tuberculosis. The situation is equally alarming in Asia, where two-thirds of the world's tuberculosis carriers live. If the AIDS epidemic continues its rapid spread, as has been the case in India and Thailand, there is a good chance the renewed outbreak of active tuberculosis will be enormous. How to react to this foreseeable disaster?

The solution is to track and treat the carriers of the bacillus before the active phase sets in. Although the treatment takes a long time—six to nine months—this would save many lives. The cost, however, would be considerable for already precarious health-care budgets: about $40 per person. In addition, the infrastructures necessary to testing, follow-up, and treatment are lacking. At times the sick are in so severe a state of poverty that they resell their week's supply of medications. Lastly, the appearance, in the United States and Europe, of tuberculosis bacillus strains resistant to current therapies has added to the concerns of patients and health-care professionals.

Discrimination and Testing

The fear of infectious diseases is a constant in history. It has always led to discrimination. Like plague, leprosy, and syphilis before it, AIDS elicits reactions of rejection of adults as well as children, in every country. Most of the time, this ostracism stems from a misunderstanding of the ways in which HIV is transmitted.

There is a wealth of examples. In an orphanage in Kenya, three HIV-negative young girls whose parents had died of AIDS were marginalized by their friends. In China, when the HIV-positive condition of an adolescent boy came to be known at school, the whole school was considered infected with AIDS. In Poland, when a civic association wanted to set up a house for HIV-positive people in the suburbs; the house was vandalized and burned. In France, a young hemophiliac boy was barred from a summer camp. In the United States another such boy was denied entry into a school.

The fact that people consider infected hemophiliacs "innocent victims" implies that the other sufferers are guilty. It is only one more step to sanctioning forms of segregation. Following this line of reasoning, Cuba interned their seropositive citizens for several years before setting up a more accommodating system. Bulgaria likewise wanted to test all their citizens. Some countries require a test or declaration on one's honor that one is seronegative, before foreigners can enter their territory for whatever purpose: tourism, business, study, political asylum. It was for this reason that the International Conference on AIDS, which was supposed to have taken place in Boston in 1992, was moved to Amsterdam, as the United States had demanded a special visa for all HIV-positive patients entering their territory.

The effectiveness of such coercive measures is more than debatable. Certain people may be seronegative and appear to be uninfected when passing through the seroconversion stage and so infect others. Moreover, solutions relying on force can only further marginalize the sick and the HIV-positive. By seeking to close its borders, a country only sends the problem elsewhere, while in any case infection will easily cross the illusory barriers one tries to set in its way. The only true forms of protection lie in information, more responsible modes of behavior, and freely consensual testing.

In the West, recommended or systematic testing has engendered numerous controversies. The unresolved problems seem even greater in underdeveloped countries. Confidentiality is not always respected in regard to serological status. Oftentimes, since there is no treatment to be offered, health-care professionals wonder what benefit there could be for the patients in knowing their status. Should one tell them or not? What is the point of upsetting already deprived people to whom one can offer nothing?

Some experiences, however, have been encouraging. In Uganda, for example, in certain villages where the seropositivity rate is as high as 30 percent, the sick are not at all excluded, but rather taken in and cared for by the whole community.

CONCERNS FOR THE FUTURE AND REASONS FOR HOPE

A vast chasm in treatments and outcomes separates the industrialized from the developing countries. In the latter, and in Africa in particular, AIDS has aggravated an already precarious health situation. There is nevertheless hope that, with the advent of this disease, the health-care structures as a whole can be made to improve.

An annual report of the World Bank indicated that in 1990,

health-care expenses were barely $6 a year per person in low-income countries (those whose annual per capita incomes were less than $635). From a health-care point of view and leaving AIDS aside, the bare minimum in care could be provided for less than $12 per person. With AIDS the figure jumps to thousands of dollars.

On the world map, such countries cover almost all of black Africa and parts of Asia such as Vietnam, Laos, and Cambodia. They all figure among the countries most infected by HIV. There AIDS has joined other great infectious diseases that have practically vanished from the West. This distressing situation demands the attention and concern of the international community, so that health care for everyone might be improved. Progress will only be made by encouraging interaction between developed and underdeveloped countries.

In 1990, also according to the World Bank, aid for health care constituted only 6 percent all international aid, that is, $4 billion, or a little less than one dollar per inhabitant in the underdeveloped countries. These figures are derisory; the international community must find a way to increase its efforts.

A worldwide effort must be made, involving all the different players—the international community, the governments of the concerned countries, and nongovernmental organizations (NGOs)—to provide the best possible prevention, care for the sick, and therapeutic research.

NGOs working in the field are sometimes more effective than national programs: they can move about more easily in certain communities—among prostitutes and drug addicts, for example. In Thailand, the Empower association has aimed its activity at prostitutes. With the help of documents, games, and videos Empower tries to explain the mutual risk involved in not using condoms with their clients. This is important, because sometimes these populations are very infected and marginalized, and the public authorities are not willing, for political reasons, to take care of them. Hence there sometimes are tensions between NGOs and governments that feel challenged by them.

In the face of the seriousness of the epidemic and the lack of resources, one must make certain choices. Health-care institutions must have the ability to take care of people already sick, prevent opportunistic infections (especially tuberculosis), and anticipate the future by limiting new infections.

Prevention remains the top priority in any attempt to limit the epidemic as long as there is no available vaccine. It requires informing and educating the population about HIV infection and the ways to protect oneself against it; but as we have seen, in every country there is a significant gap between understanding and changes in behavior.

It is a long and demanding task that lies ahead. An effort must be made to make condom use among men systematic and widespread, and to persuade them to limit their number of partners. But women also have a central role to play in the prevention of this epidemic. They are often in a situation that leaves them no power of decision. This is why it is necessary to encourage that women be taught about their bodies and sexuality, in order to give them a better chance of becoming agents of prevention both for their partners and for their children. This education could go hand in hand with a mastery of fertility, given that in many cultures feminine and tribal power are linked to the number of children they have.

Quaternary ammonium spermicides have demonstrated a certain effectiveness in locally inactivating the virus, but they induce some irritation of the vaginal mucous membrane. They could therefore have the paradoxical effect of facilitating HIV infection. It is thus necessary to promote research aimed at developing derivatives that are less irritating, more active, and have a broader range of effects, so they can be used against other sexually transmissible diseases as well. This would be an effective means of prevention. WHO is actively supporting this sort of research.

Children and adolescents must likewise be informed and educated, to avoid future infections. This must be done first and foremost in the schools, but unfortunately fewer and fewer children are going to school because of parental illness and the precariousness of the family.

AIDS sufferers and HIV-positive people, for the most part, do not currently receive adequate care, since antiviral treatments are very expensive. It would be advisable to aim at least treating opportunistic infections, for there are recognized effective treatments for these; all the players in the health-care process must participate in these efforts, to ensure that medications are effectively administered. On the whole, therapeutic research must do its utmost to find inexpensive solutions without ruling out the possible usefulness of traditional healing medicine.

International efforts and programs have thus focused more, in third world countries, on the prevention and control of the epidemic than on the realities of the sick and the care they need, which in the industrialized countries have instead constituted a major priority. It nevertheless seems that in spite of the difficulties, especially the epidemic's impact on development on the African continent, there are reasons for hope. The Africans themselves are beginning to be aware of the problem, and the richer nations seem committed to helping them. Recently, six different U.N. agencies have decided to combine their efforts into a single organization, called UNAIDS, while remaining closely associated with WHO in Geneva. Today there seems to be a genuine, worldwide will to arrest this scourge, and to increase and combine efforts so that all may benefit from more effective prevention and care.

Epilogue

◦ *In* the last few years, an important turning point has been reached in AIDS treatment. While complete recovery from infection has not yet been achieved, the development of triple-drug therapies, especially the use of protease inhibitors, has made it possible to decrease the level of virus in the body and at least to stabilize it for a rather long period; as a result, fewer and fewer patients die of opportunistic infections and many resume their normal lives.

These advancements almost exclusively involve patients in developed countries. Worldwide, however, nothing has been resolved and it would be foolish to think that the problem is now over. The epidemic continues to rage in Africa, Asia, and South America, fueled by civil wars and poverty. To close our eyes to this—to say that it is, after all, a misfortune only affecting the third world—would be a grave mistake.

Our world is becoming increasingly globalized; national economies are interdependent; tourism is spreading to the far corners of the world. In addition, secondary epidemics, caused by highly contagious germs, could occur in millions of immunosuppressed individuals, and they would spare no one.

AIDS, therefore, must be defeated, and it can only be defeated on a worldwide scale. This objective can be realized, but we shall need time and an unflagging will.

What is to be done?

1. *We must continue to develop new means of prevention through information, and to change modes of behavior.* We must inform and keep informing, especially the young.

We must remain aware and teach the new generations, at school and at home, that at birth we are given a biological capital, a glorious but limited, fragile thing, and that we must adapt our behavior accordingly. Sex is very important in life, but it is not everything, and just as we must restrict our diet to avoid becoming obese, likewise we should limit all sexual excess. These messages should be adapted according to each cultural context and ethnic group.

It is also clear that an improvement in economic conditions in the developing countries, and the possibility of breaking the circle of prostitution and migrant labor, would favor a decline in the transmission of the virus. But these are long-term goals.

2. *We must continue to develop research.* We have already learned a great deal about the virus and the illness, and have been able to apply this new knowledge in spectacular ways, as in the ultrasensitive tests for diagnosis and monitoring, and in the use of highly potent inhibitors of the virus.

But triple-drug therapies have not solved everything. There are still some concerns as regards the latent persistence of the virus, the long-term development of cancers, the appearance of mutations of the virus resistant to all known treatments, and the development of a residual illness independent of the virus.

To repeat, only by making available a preventive, safe vaccine that can be given to children, and by combining this with prevention campaigns, will we be able to eradicate the epidemic and perhaps one day stamp out the virus.

This goal, as we have seen, is within our reach, so long as we can combine the creativity of researchers, the will of politicians, and adequate financial support. We must also realize that the investments made in AIDS research can also be highly beneficial for the treatment and prevention of much more common diseases. Studying the phenomena of oxidative stress, the immune mechanisms developed by the body against viruses and cancers, and the role of retroviruses we already have inside us (endogenous retroviruses) may help us to understand and overcome such diseases as multiple sclerosis, Alzheimer's, atherosclerosis, and cancers—all those chronic diseases that afflict us as we age and finally drag us into decline and an early death.

3. *We must make these advancements available to all.* It is essential that patients in poor countries have access to the new treatments. Naturally, the exhorbitant cost of these treatments is an obstacle, but it is not the only obstacle. There are others of equal importance: the lack of adequate laboratory services to measure the viral load and other parameters of the immune system, the difficulty of obtaining the strict compliance of patients, not to mention the cultural obstacle of treating an infection that takes a long time to manifest itself in visible signs of illness.

In my opinion, triple-drug therapies will only become practical if they can be given over a limited time. Today the treatment must be given over indefinitely. If the patient stops treatment, the virus resumes multiplying and the viral load increases.

The ideal would therefore be to find a treatment that could be given over a period of six to twelve months, like the treatment for active tuberculosis with antibiotics, and that could perhaps eradicate viral multiplication or at least maintain it at a very low, harmless level. This is based on the assumption that the immune system can continue and finish the work begun by the antiviral drugs.

The search for complementary treatments, including those

belonging to the traditional pharmacopoeia of Africa and Asia, is therefore an absolute necessity.

That is why, to help bring about such changes, it is necessary to work in those places where the epidemic has spread and to create research laboratories in Africa and Asia. A few already exist. These centers, which are on the same level as American and European laboratories, should also pay attention to local approaches that have a solid scientific basis, such as traditional plant-based medications. In the face of a scourge such as this, one must leave no stone unturned, even that of empirical medicine. Lastly, such laboratories should be able to serve as logistical bases for future vaccine trials. Some will say this approach hardly makes sense, when such countries are wanting in everything and teeming with parasitosis, malaria, tuberculosis, and malnutrition. Quite to the contrary, it could have a positive effect on the other infrastructures, with the fight against AIDS serving as a catalyst for developing coherent health policies.

A major international effort is thus needed to create these structures in the developing countries. The effort must be both public—requiring the unified collaboration of the richest governments and international financial institutions with the governments of the poorer countries—and private. And by way of example, I would like in conclusion to describe my own initiatives this regard.

Since the mid-1980s, I have realized that my position as a pioneer researcher whose team first isolated the virus, and the notoriety I have achieved in this domain, could help me to reach beyond my research activities and contribute to resolving the problem of AIDS worldwide. Thus in 1993, in conjunction with the director general of UNESCO, Federico Mayor, I created the World Foundation for AIDS Research and Prevention. The goals of this foundation, which is Swiss by law but currently has offices in France, kindly made available to us by UNESCO, are to contribute to research, especially vaccine research, to develop treatments accessible to patients in the Southern Hemisphere, and to provide information and education in conjunction with UNESCO and UNAIDS.

How will we realize these goals? Through the creation of a network of integrated bioclinical research centers bringing together researchers and clinicians treating asymptomatic patients. These centers are now being created in the countries most affected by the epidemic, in both the Northern and Southern Hemispheres. Scientific information and the researchers themselves circulate freely through these centers, while the laboratory methods have been standardized, with the result that the research potential of the whole has been vastly multiplied.

At the moment, three such centers have so far been created. One is in Paris, in a private hospital, Saint-Joseph Hospital, thanks to the generosity of donors to a French "telethon" and some public funds. The second is in Abidjan (Ivory Coast) and was established with the help of the Ivory Coast government and private and public donors. The third is in the New York area, at Queens College, and is being set up thanks to private donors and public aid from the State and City of New York. A first laboratory, working in close connection with the hospitals of the greater New York area, is in operation, and will be followed by the construction of a larger center.

Other centers are planned for Bangkok (Thailand), Pretoria (South Africa), and Latin America, and other European and American branches are in the process of being established. In this way, the ambitious plan of founding a world institute "without walls"—or rather, with multiple walls—is taking shape; it will be devoted entirely to AIDS at first, but later will naturally be able to devote its energies to attacking other diseases as well. This network is not, of course, a ghetto, but is entirely open to the outside world, actively collaborating with academic laboratories and biotechnology and pharmaceutical companies.

It is our hope that this initiative, which could never have been realized without the aid of enthusiastic collaborators and colleagues, will contribute, in conjunction with other endeavors, toward the earliest possible eradication of this epidemic. We will show that humanity is not only capable of harnessing the energy of atoms, of communicating at the speed of light, and exploring the planets and stars, but can also harness its own development and take action against the biological factors that may threaten its very existence.

Notes

=

Introduction

1. *Global Summary of HIV/AIDS Epidemic* (UNAIDS and WHO, Geneva, December 1998).

Chapter 1

1. L forms are derived from some bacteria that reversibly lose their rigid walls under the effect of penicillin.

   But in nature, there are also small bacteria living without walls, which have probably lost forever the genetic information for synthesis of the wall components. The first agent of this group was described in 1898 by two researchers of the Pasteur Institute, Nocard and E. Roux, who also showed its association with a bovine pneumonia. Similar agents found associated with some other animal diseases were then called PPLO for peri-pneumonia-like organisms, before being renamed mycoplasmas. Mycoplasmas are the tiniest autonomous organisms and can pass through filters that retain normal bacteria.

2. Further research conducted at the Rockefeller University in New York by Jim Darnell and David Baltimore would confirm these findings on another RNA virus, the poliomyelitis virus. But I was the first to bring them to light, and it was with great pride that I signed, with Kingsley Sanders, a groundbreaking article in the journal *Nature* on the replicative form of the RNA of the mouse encephalomyocarditis virus.

3. There were two kinds of viruses: small DNA viruses, such as mouse polyoma and the SV40 monkey virus; and the RNA tumor viruses that

were known to cause leukemias and sarcomas in chickens and rodents. We now call such RNA viruses retroviruses, but at the time their mode of replication was not known.

4. In 1969, I gave a presentation on the replication of carcinogenic viruses to the conference on comparative leukemias held in Cherry Hill, N.J., outside of Philadelphia. In my talk, I explicitly entertained this enzyme hypothesis along with others.

5. Hill and Hillova sent their work to the journal *Nature,* but their paper was not published until a year later. Meanwhile, Philippe Vigier and I achieved the same results, showing in addition that this infectious viral DNA was associated with chromosomal DNA and thus well integrated.

6. Earlier, Alice Golde and Raymond Latarjet had been the first in France to separate, using radiation, the "cancer" gene from other genes of the retrovirus.

7. Our means for determining the biochemistry of transmembrane proteins were very limited, and the result was something of a failure. I then turned my attention to the change of membrane properties due to protein phosphorylation (in which phosphate ions are added to molecules). With the help of a visiting Italian researcher, Giuseppe Piedimonte, I found significant phosphorylating activity associated with the outer membrane of the mitochondria of cancer cells. Understanding the role mitochondria play in cancer goes back to the 1920s. The German physiologist Otto Warburg then observed that the mitochondria of cancer cells function poorly and that these cells tend to use as an energy source another chain of glucose transformation, without oxygen, which allows them to survive and multiply even when conditions of blood vascularization (the process of forming blood vessels) and hence oxygenation are mediocre. But is this metabolic change a cause, as Warburg thought, or a consequence?

8. The Japanese named this virus ATLV, for adult T-cell leukemia virus, but they later accepted the term given by Robert Gallo.

9. Contrary to reports by some American sources, Françoise Barré-Sinoussi did not work with Robert Gallo on HTLV and did not learn any of the techniques for growing T lymphocytes in culture. Nor did she have any contact in Gallo's laboratory with the group working on HTLV.

Chapter 2

1. The immune system, in humans, relies on organs (lymph, nodes, spleen, intestine, and bone marrow) that produce white cells, or lym-

phocytes, whose task is to defend the body against outside aggressors. T lymphocytes (so called because they are dependent on the thymus for maturation) are subdivided into several groups. T4 lymphocytes, in particular, play the role of orchestra director, stimulating the other cells of the immune system. The signals they emit activate the T8 lymphocytes, whose task is to kill the cells infected by pathogenic agents. They also activate the B lymphocytes, which secret antibodies and neutralize infectious agents.

2. Lymphoma is a malignant tumor affecting the lymphoid tissues, that is, the constituent of the immune system that produces lymphocytes.

3. A laminar flow hood has an air-circulation curtain that prevents any germs or spores from entering or leaving the area in which they are being manipulated. The operator is thus protected from any contamination, as are the cells or viral cultures that might be contaminated by microorganisms carried by the operator.

4. Lymph-node lymphocytes are embedded in a rather hard stroma, or connective-tissue matrix; to free them, one must apply appropriate pressure, though not too hard, since that would destroy the cells. To do this, I used a Dounce homogenizer, which consists of a glass ball forming a plunger and sliding inside a glass tube, and is generally used to prepare the cells of soft tissues, such as the liver. To favor dissociation, I cut the lymph tissue into little cubes with a pair of curved scissors.

5. In fact, we know today that this protein A, which has the property of binding antibodies, activates lymphocytes thanks only to certain impurities it contains, which act as superantigens. The activation produced is rather mild, without overly agglutinating the cells; protein A activates all types of lymphocytes.

6. For a description of B and T lymphocytes, see note 1 for Chapter 2.

7. I initially obtained this factor in a nonpurified state from Robert Gallo in 1980. It was used for growing T lymphocytes from patients with breast cancer, and had run out several months before I started the AIDS virus experiments. For the latter, I obtained more of the same factor from Didier Fradellizi, who worked in Jean Dausset's Laboratory at the St. Louis Hospital. Today, interleukin 2 is obtained in purified state from bacteria containing the human gene that codes for its synthesis.

8. The reason for adding anti-interferon serum was to neutralize the interferon synthesized by the lymphocytes in response to viral infection. This interferon would otherwise decrease multiplication of the virus, making the latter more difficult to isolate.

9. The lymphocytes of newborns are devoid of infection by certain herpes viruses and are more easily transformed by HTLV than are adult lymphocytes.

10. Lentiviruses are one of the three subfamilies of retroviruses, which also include viruses that cause slowly developing noncancerous illness in sheep, goats and horses.

11. One of the best-known lentiviruses is the Visna virus, which causes pneumonia or encephalitis in sheep. In the 1950s, it was the cause of an epidemic in Iceland.

12. As for patients with advanced AIDS, only 20 to 40 percent had antibodies detectable by this test. This figure would rise to 90 percent in April 1984, with an improved lab test.

13. On the same day in Europe, the Pasteur Institute submitted the first patent request for an AIDS diagnostic test based on the detection of antibodies of LAV.

14. Mika Popovic, of Gallo's laboratory, signed an agreement that the specimens received would not be used for commercial purposes.

15. The liquid medium for growing cells is usually kept at a neutral pH by a bicarbonate buffer maintained by an enriched concentration of carbon dioxide (CO_2) in the air surrounding the medium. Most laboratories use large incubators in which this enriched air continuously circulates. Culture flasks or petri dishes must therefore not be hermetically sealed in order to have access to this CO_2-air mixture. As a result, aerosols, and therefore viruses, could conceivably pass from flask to flask. A culture of virus with high growth potential could thus contaminate a culture infected with a virus of lower growth potential. Aware of this problem, I have always used culture flasks that are tightly stoppered after being gassed with the CO_2-air mixture. But the LAI and BRU mass cultures were not always made under these conditions, making possible contamination of one by the other.

16. The abbreviation LAV/BRU/MT2 refers to the LAV BRU strain cultivated on T lymphocytes and passaged (grown and harvested) twice on precursor cells from bone marrow.

17. The BRU/MT2 virus grew equally well on the original CEM line, and two months of patient work helped it to improve. David Klatzmann enriched the cells that were most expressing the CD4 receptor, the receptor of the virus. Then Jacqueline Gruest cloned the cells in agar, each cell forming a colony whose capacity for producing the virus was

then tested. The clones producing the greatest quantities of virus were given over to Diagnostics Pasteur, in autumn 1984. This line was in fact more productive than Gallo's H9 cell line. Moreover, compared with the H9 cells, it expressed much less of the cellular molecules (HLA) that are incorporated in the viral envelope and can give rise to false-positive antibody reactions. Eventually, knowing what the genes of the virus are would enable us, through genetic engineering, to produce the viral proteins and to achieve the state of perfection of the current detection tests.

18. In San Francisco, Jay Levy's lab had also isolated an AIDS virus entirely independently of LAV/HTLV-III, and this virus was sequenced under the direction of the young molecular biologist Paul Luciw.

19. The patent request for our HIV test was submitted to the U.S. Patent Office on December 5, 1983, while Gallo's was submitted on April 23, 1984. The Patent Office granted authorization for Gallo's test on May 28, 1985, while our request had not yet even been examined. Genetic Systems, Diagnostics Pasteur's partner in the United States, did not receive the license for marketing our test in the United States until February 18, 1986. By this time it was clear that the virus used by Gallo and Abbott for the diagnostic AIDS test was the LAV that the Pasteur Institute had isolated.

20. To develop our diagnostic test in the United States, in 1984 we had chosen the company Genetic Systems, at the time a small biotechnology company in Seattle, founded by Robert Nowinski. Thus began an exemplary collaboration that made possible the development of more sensitive detection tests, called "second-generation" with peptides. Further research also made possible the first identification of a monoclonal antibody that neutralized a variable region (the V3 loop of the virus envelope).

21. The agreement signed in July 1994 was financially weighted in the Pasteur Institute's favor, given the acknowledgment by the American authorities of their improper use, for commercial ends, of the virus isolated in France.

Chapter 3

1. Hervé Guibert, *A l'ami qui ne m'a pas sauvé la vie* [To the Friend Who Did Not Save My Life] (Paris: Gallimard, 1990), pp. 15–16, "Folio" collection. Passage translated by Stephen Sartarelli.

2. This is a glycoprotein (hence the abbreviation "gp"); that is, it consists of sugar-based chains attached to a protein backbone.

3. It has been shown recently that such "weak" viral strains preferentially use a specific coreceptor, present on lymphocytes and macrophages, called CCR5.

4. Tuberculosis is caused by the Koch bacillus, *Mycobacterium tuberculosis.* According to the World Health Organization, in 1992, 1.7 billion individuals were infected with this microbe. In industrialized countries, thanks to an amelioration of living conditions and effective treatment, the incidence of tuberculosis had been decreasing for thirty years. This trend has been reversing itself since 1985. The problem of tuberculosis is now becoming even more acute with the appearance of new bacillus strains that are resistant to antibiotics. In Africa, where it strikes one out of two HIV-infected patients, it is generally a reactivated form of an old tuberculosis. Extrapulmonary forms (those occurring outside the lungs) that had not been seen for years are now developing again. The multiple antibiotic treatment usually lasts nine months.

Pulmonary pneumocystosis is caused by the protozoan *Pneumocystis carinii.* The germ enters the lung cells and causes severe pneumonia.

Toxoplasmosis is caused by *Toxoplasma gondii,* an intracellular protozoan whose favorite target is the brain, where it creates abscesses. In less frequent cases, it affects the eyes and the lungs.

5. Kaposi's sarcoma is a tumor originating from the abnormal growth of the cells that form blood vessel walls. This seems to be caused by a virus in the herpes family, called human herpes virus 8 (HHV-8), which often infects homosexual men with multiple partners. This virus is rare in the general population and more frequent in Africa.

Lymphoma is a potentially malignant tumor of the lymph glands. Half of the cases of B cell lymphoma have been shown to be caused by the Epstein-Barr virus (EBV), and it has been linked to Burkitt's lymphoma. As with all tumors, lymphoma goes through several phases. The initial proliferation phase seems linked to the direct action of EBV genes; then there is a chromosomal modification that brings about the overexpression of an oncogene and the emergence of a fast-growing tumor cell. Actually, most of us have cells of this type somewhere in our tissues, but their proliferation is permanently repressed by our immune system, especially by cytotoxic T8 cells. It is the weakening of this defense, indirectly due to the weaking of T4 cells by HIV, that allows the tumor to emerge.

Chapter 4

1. Mirko D. Grmek, *Histoire du SIDA,* new ed. (Paris: Payot, 1990).
2. More recently, three more isolates have been obtained from chimpanzees, including two from Cameroon. These isolates are very close to the major branch (M) of HIV-1, reinforcing the hypothesis of a transmission from chimpanzees to humans, although the reverse cannot be absolutely excluded.
3. Grmek.

Chapter 8

1. In 1998–1999, two phase 3 trials were started, in the United States and Thailand.

Index